During the post–World War II period, a pattern emerged in several European countries: centralized and concerted political regulation of the economy based on Keynesian policies, the development of the welfare state and moderately successful attempts at tripartite agreements. This pattern underwent a serious crisis in the 1980s, however, and in the view of many observers was replaced by a far-reaching deregulation of the economy.

In contrast to this view, Professor Regini argues that social and political institutions have by no means lost their ability to structure economic activities. They have, in fact, shaped the different ways in which the European economies have adjusted to market conditions. Regini argues that while it is wrong to see deregulation as a general trend taking place in formerly institutionally regulated economies, the relevant institutions have changed. A pattern of 'micro-social' regulation of European economies has emerged as a potential replacement for the 'macro-political' one, though the boundaries between the two forms of regulation remain quite uncertain. This volume discusses the conditions under which a change from a macro to a micro form takes place, as well as the features of the emerging pattern.

Uncertain boundaries

CAMBRIDGE STUDIES IN COMPARATIVE POLITICS

General editor
PETER LANGE   Duke University

Associate editors
ELLEN COMISSO   University of California, San Diego
PETER HALL   Harvard University
JOEL MIGDAL   University of Washington
HELEN MILNER   Columbia University
SIDNEY TARROW   Cornell University
RONALD ROGOWSKI   University of California, Los Angeles

Uncertain boundaries
The social and political construction
of European economies

MARINO REGINI

CAMBRIDGE
UNIVERSITY PRESS

Published by the Press Syndicate of the University of Cambridge
The Pitt Building, Trumpington Street, Cambridge CB2 1RP
40 West 20th Street, New York, NY 10011-4211, USA
10 Stamford Road, Oakleigh, Melbourne 3166, Australia

Originally published in Italian as *Confini mobili*
© 1991 Società Editrice Il Mulino, Bologna

© Cambridge University Press 1995

First published 1995

Printed in the United States of America

Library of Congress Cataloging-in-Publication Data
Regini, Marino, 1943–

Uncertain boundaries : the social and political construction of
European economies / Marino Regini.

p.   cm. – (Cambridge studies in comparative politics)

Includes index.

ISBN 0-521-47371-3

1. Europe – Economic policy. 2. Europe – Economic conditions – 1945–
3. Europe – Politics and government – 1945– I. Title. II. Series.

HC240.R334   1995

330.12'6'094 – dc20   94-21946
                                                          CIP

A catalog record for this book is available from the British Library.

ISBN 0-521-47371-3 Hardback

Contents

Preface

This book does not set out the results of a specific research study, nor does it present a fully developed theory. It is the outcome, instead, of the accretion, so to speak, of analytical insights derived from various research studies conducted in recent years by the present writer and from the theoretical reflections that accompanied them. The overall analytical framework proposed here was by no means clear when these studies were carried out and when these reflections were developed. I have found it necessary, in fact, to re-examine them carefully, to complete them with further analysis and to seek out the connections among them. The structure of the book emerged only gradually as the implications of each piece of analysis for the others, and the interconnections among them, became clear.

Why this overall analytical framework was not initially clear, and indeed at first sight may seem arbitrary to the reader, warrants some explanation. The reason lies in the increasingly sharp division of scientific labour – and the scant incentive to scholars who wish to overcome the specializations of their disciplines – with regard to both tools of analysis and the topics that have traditionally been addressed by the discipline. As will become immediately clear to anyone familiar with the contemporary social sciences, the topics examined in Part I of this book are conventionally the concern of political economy, to some extent of political sociology, and of political science. The topics addressed in Part II pertain to the sociology of work, to industrial economics and to industrial relations. For this reason, the literature, theories and schemes of analysis relevant to the first part of the book are seldom extended to the issues dealt with in the second. Yet I have gradually come to believe that the two areas of inquiry are so closely connected that failure to take systematic account of their interconnections (or, to anticipate the expression that I shall use later in the book, the lack of integration between the macro- and micro-levels on which the economy is regulated) produces serious analytical distortions.

Part I discusses the reasons for the rise, the advantages and disadvantages and the decline of what I call the model of 'concerted and centralized political regulation' of the market economies. This is a form of macro-regulation where the state and large interest organizations fulfil the vital task of allocating resources in order to counteract the socially undesirable outcomes of the operation of the market, although this continues to be the dominant economic institution. The ingredients of this model – Keynesian policies, the welfare state, concertation with organized interests – have been subjected to ample analysis in the literature, but they have not always been treated as parts of a larger whole, and they have rarely been examined in terms of their relationship with the underlying micro-level at which economic actors operate.

After sustaining the extraordinary economic development enjoyed by the West for almost half a century, in the 1980s this model entered a phase of decline. Yet contrary to the view of the majority of analysts of this first group of phenomena, the crisis of this historically specific form of the regulation of the economy did not impede the ability of political and social institutions to structure economic behaviour. To anticipate my argument in Part II, the economic adjustment that took place during the 1980s was by no means based on a simple return to the 'free operation of the market'. In several European countries it took advantage of institutionally dense situations which conditioned actors' strategies and therefore the ways in which their economies were restructured.

An institutionally regulated economy was not replaced by a deregulated one. Only the forms of regulation and the main institutions were changed. From macro-political, the regulation of economic activities became predominantly micro-social. And the search for consensus that had characterized the former was again a vital ingredient of the latter – albeit, as we shall see, in a different form. Yet to what extent forms of micro-social regulation (which I examine in Part II) may constitute a stable alternative to the concerted and centralized political regulation of the economy (which is the theme of Part I), and to what extent new points of equilibrium must be found between micro and macro, is the principal, and as yet unanswered, question.

A book such as the one outlined here, of course, reuses insights from previous research and analysis. Nevertheless, this book is anything but a mere collection of essays; indeed, the large majority of its chapters and sections have never been published previously, and those few which have already appeared in print have been substantially revised, reworked and, above all, rethought to fit into the analytical framework I mentioned above. Moreover, a book such as this necessarily includes chapters – like those in Part I – that systematize, and relate to the book's central issues, analyses which are by now well established and widely discussed in the literature, and other chapters that explore much more uncharted terrain in order to advance interpretations which only future research can verify and enrich.

Acknowledgements

I have several long-standing intellectual debts to repay, for this book stems from prolonged contact with different scientific settings. These debts, therefore, are collective rather than individual, and I gratefully acknowledge them here.

First of all, the analysis in Part I owes a great deal to the journal *Stato e Mercato*, which has played a major role in developing the interdisciplinary approach that goes by the name of 'political economy' and in whose columns the relationships between economy, social conditions and political-institutional arrangements have received searching scrutiny. The periodic debates on the editorial board of *Stato e Mercato* – in which I have always had the good fortune to participate – have provided me with unique opportunities to develop and test my ideas. I am indebted in particular to Michele Salvati, Massimo Paci, Arnaldo Bagnasco, Carlo Trigilia, Philippe Schmitter and Gösta Esping-Andersen, but my thanks extend to all the other members of the editorial board.

With regard to the topics explored in Part II, I have found fruitful opportunities to discuss these at Ires Lombardia, a small research institute which for a number of years has operated as a true scientific community in which personal relationships are inseparable from professional ones and the contribution of individuals is difficult to distinguish from collective endeavour. This community, enlivened by the presence of Rosalba Moroni, comprises numerous people with whom my intellectual contacts have been intense and enduring: principally Ida Regalia, with whom I have shared so many ideas and work projects, but also Alessandro Arrighetti, Paolo Perulli, Emilio Reyneri, Antonio Chiesi, Paolo Santi and all the other members of the institute who in some measure have helped with the intellectual enterprise set out in this book.

Those who teach and carry out a large part of their research at universities inevitably owe a considerable debt to their students and colleagues. During the period in which this book was gestating, I taught at two different universities: on the Faculty of Political Sciences of the University of Milan and the

Faculty of Sociology of the University of Trento. As regards the former, I wish to thank those colleagues with whom I had the most frequent opportunities for stimulating discussion, notably Bianca Beccalli, Marco Maraffi, Alberto Martinelli and, above all, Gloria Regonini. As regards the latter, I shall restrict myself to recalling my discussions, sometimes heated but always marked by mutual respect, with my late colleague and friend Guido Romagnoli.

In addition, there is another kind of scientific setting, one which corresponds to no formal institution but which I am duty-bound to mention because it has been just as important in the writing of this book as the others. I refer to the international community of scholars of political economy who, through joint initiatives, informal discussion and in some cases direct collaboration, have contributed their valuable comments and criticisms, thereby providing me with constant verification of my analysis. I especially thank Peter Lange and Chuck Sabel, with whom I have co-ordinated two collective projects with a profound impact on this book (Lange and Regini 1989; Regini and Sabel 1989), as well as David Soskice and Wolfgang Streeck, to whose ideas I was largely reacting when I wrote the conclusions to this book.

Although it is not entirely true, I shall follow the customary practice of adding that none of these people is in any way responsible for what I have written in the pages that follow.

Finally, I wish to thank Adrian Belton for helping me with the English translation of the text.

Introduction: the shifting boundaries between market, politics and society

The history of the development of capitalism in the West, and of the organization of the economic system consequent upon it, evidences the progressive predominance of the market over other institutions. As well as being the chief mechanism for the regulation of economic activity, the market is conventionally regarded as an institution whose laws have come to permeate broad areas of social life, supplanting the norms produced by the state and the community. In short, when we think of the growth of capitalism, we often think of the penetration of the market – and of the principles of competition and exchange on which it is based – into economic and social relationships which were previously governed by other principles, notably solidarity and hierarchy or authority.

The founders of the social sciences based various of the themes most central to their thought on this vision of the market. Suffice it to mention Weber, who ascribed great importance to the principle of rationality, which arose from the necessity for calculation and predictability imposed by the market, and which also came to dominate social life and the political system by embodying itself in the bureaucracy. Or Durkheim, for whom the demise of 'mechanical solidarity' and the rise of 'organic solidarity' was based on the division of labour, and hence on exchange – the predominant criterion for the allocation of resources in the market. Or Marx, for whom capitalism reduced the relationships among individuals to market relationships *tout court* and labour to a commodity, to a 'labour force' which was demanded and supplied on a market, the labour market.

A traditional reading of the relationship between economy, politics and society in the social sciences thus stresses the effects exerted by the organization of the economy – dominated as it is by the laws of the market – on social relationships in the broad sense. In other words, it highlights the spillovers into the spheres of social and political life of a mode of regulating the economy which is based mainly on the market.

There is, however, an alternative (almost reverse) interpretation, one which has gained wide currency in the social sciences and which is today confronted by theoretical and political problems of greater importance. This interpretation draws together diversified strands of thought whose only common feature is their focus on the role that social and political institutions can play in an economic system in which the market has a central, but not exclusive function. The thesis that the organization of economic life, even in a period of triumphant capitalism, can never be wholly restricted to the market (which in any case is not always able to generate optimal allocative outcomes) is by now so widespread as to be almost a commonplace. From this thesis derive, however, very different approaches to the analysis of the role of nonmarket institutions in the economy.

A highly reductionist position, in both analytical and prescriptive terms, is the view that confines the various social and political institutions to a marginal role in the regulation of the economic system; that is, their role is simply to intervene when it is necessary to compensate for the insufficient development or 'failure' of the market.

The classical strand of political economy instead concentrates (with various value judgements) on the 'political regulation' of the market – that is, when the state, often in agreement with large interest organizations, is entrusted with crucial tasks of resource allocation in order to counteract the socially undesirable outcomes of the market's operation. These tasks mainly involve the readjustment of distorted economic development and compensation for the inequalities of income and power that the market produces.

There is a third role that social and political institutions may perform in the economic system, one that again involves interference in the market – not, however, in this case to readjust it or to compensate for its undesirable effects, but to shape its very functioning. By structuring the options available to market participants, social and political institutions induce them – sometimes explicitly and deliberately, sometimes as an unintended consequence of their action – to pursue some goals rather than others. By doing so, they help the market to produce outcomes which its participants, as actors rationally motivated to satisfy their immediate interests, would be unable to achieve on their own.

This book adopts the less traditional interpretation of the relationship between economy, politics and society. That is to say, it concentrates on the role of social and political institutions in the functioning (or in the dysfunctioning) of the economic system, and not vice versa.

Against this background, the phenomena studied by the classical strand of political economy were undoubtedly crucial for half of this century (approximately from the 1930s to the early 1980s). Their crisis – or their declining

importance – in the past decade has induced many social scientists to cele-
brate the wholesale restoration of the market, now entirely untrammelled by
interference and constraint by other institutions. The demise of a model of the
regulation of the economic system (which we may call the 'concerted and
centralized political regulation' of the economy and which is analysed in Part
I) has often been mistaken for the demise of political economy *tout court*.

This, however, is not the case. The crisis of this model has coincided with
greater awareness of the role performed by other forms of social regulation –
ranging from community networks in which shared values predominate, to
bargaining among organized interests – in conditioning the workings of the
market. Above all, the social and institutional factors operating at the micro-
level (i.e., at the level of the production site or the local economic-social
organization) have become increasingly important in encouraging or impeding
change in the economic system by structuring its actors' interests. This accounts for the title given to Part II: 'The Micro-Social Regulation of Economic Adjustment'. These tendencies are still amorphous and difficult to decipher,
and when analysing them one can offer only tentative conjecture rather than
solidly based explanation. Nevertheless, the third perspective just outlined of
the role of social and political institutions – namely, that they structure the
options of market participants so that they pursue some goals and behaviours
rather than others – becomes more persuasive. Consequently, we can speak of
new ways in which society conditions the economy rather than of the further
autonomization of the economic subsystem by society itself.

The debate on the relationships between state and market in regulating
economic activities has a long history. In the social sciences after the Second
World War, such debate was particularly intense in the 1960s with the publica-
tion of the influential book by Andrew Shonfield (1965), which showed that,
in several European countries, the state had assumed a role of considerable
importance in the economy. The expansion of Keynesian policies and the
welfare state, and the growth of the public sector and a mixed economy,
appeared in those years to be enduring phenomena, perhaps irreversible, and
they were looked upon with a certain degree of favour by economists and
social scientists. Even those who criticized – particularly during the 1970s –
the appropriation of public resources by social groups or even the 'colonization of the state' by private interests, or again the emergence of neocorporatist
forms of public policy-making, only stressed the other side of the same
phenomenon, which was by now accepted as inevitable: namely, the increasing importance of the state in the allocation of economic resources.

Nevertheless, it was only later that Shonfield's observations managed to
break down the disciplinary barriers between economists, sociologists and

political scientists, so that when a number of scholars finally decided to 'bring the state back into' their analyses (Skocpol 1985), the phenomenon was already in decline.[1] Indeed, many countries were displaying opposite trends.

In the 1980s, in fact, the reverse phenomenon seemed to arise; that is, to use the title of a book edited by Charles Maier (1987), the boundaries of the political began to shrink. The deregulation of the economy came to occupy a central place in ideological debate and, to some extent, on the political agenda (especially in the United States and Great Britain). This was the consequence of three groups of phenomena of major importance: first, those considered to be the 'perverse effects' of Keynesian policies and of the expansion of the welfare state (the fiscal crisis, the overload of demand on the state, the decommodification of the work-force, etc.; see the third section of Chapter 1); second, the new constraints imposed by increased international competition, which meant that the national economies could no longer afford to operate within acceptable margins of inefficiency and suboptimal performance (see Chapter 6); third, changed power relations in the market, and in several cases also in the political arena, to the detriment of labour or the Left in general.

For these reasons, many political economists engaged in analysing changes in the regulation of economic activities are prompted to ask the following straightforward question: In the regulation of these activities, has there or has there not been a reduction in the role of the state compared with that of the market over the past fifteen years? That is to say, has the effective retreat of the state, so widely predicted (or hoped for), actually come about, or has that system of widespread intervention described almost thirty years ago by Shonfield, and subsequently by many other commentators, substantially persisted?

It should be pointed out that, by framing the question in these terms, certain analysts – even more so many protagonists of political debate – are led to believe that state and market are sharply distinct and competing regulatory institutions. They therefore tend to analyse (and more often to denounce) 'interferences' in their respective spheres of competence rather than seek to understand the ways in which the two institutions actually combine. Or they concentrate on presumed general trends, such as the retreat of the state or the revival of the market, instead of examining ongoing changes in the mix between them. Moreover, they also entirely ignore the role of other regulatory institutions (community and associations).

Often, the meaning itself of 'regulation of the economic system' is reduced to that of state intervention as opposed to the workings of the market. In this book, by drawing on the richer and less reductionist traditions of political economy, I adopt a broader definition. By 'regulation of the economy' I mean the various modes by which that set of activities and inter-actor relationships associated with the production and distribution of economic resources is co-ordinated, these resources are allocated and the related conflicts, real or potential, are structured – that is, prevented or resolved. Following a long tradition of study (Polanyi 1944; Williamson 1975; Lindblom 1977; Ouchi 1977), we may say that these various modes or forms of regulation are the following: state regulation based on the principle of authority; market regulation based on exchange; communitarian regulation based on solidarity; and, according to Streeck and Schmitter (1985), associational regulation based on inter- and intraorganizational concertation.

In sum, first, state and market should not be analysed as regulatory institutions necessarily antithetical to each other – so that when one increases in importance the other correspondingly declines – because there are several areas of economic activity which base their operations on a complex interweaving of the two. Second, state and market are not the only institutions that regulate the economic system. Third, 'regulation of the economy' is synonymous neither with state intervention nor with centralized political regulation, as has often been assumed; it is a concept which includes other forms taken by the co-ordination of activities and relationships, by the allocation of resources and by the structuring of conflicts – forms which operate at the micro-level under the influence of other social institutions. I now briefly examine each of these three points.

First, studies conducted in several countries on various types of economic and social policy – that is, on areas of economic activities and relationships at least potentially subject to state intervention – have shown combinations of state and market which vary greatly from one area to another. There are few activities and relationships associated with the production and distribution of resources in which either the state or the market, or some other regulatory institution, entirely predominates. Their co-presence is not an exception which engenders instability and conflict, but the normal state of affairs in many areas of economic activity. Among other things, it is this mix that accounts for the opaque but constant nature of changes in regulatory processes. These changes often appear as marginal shifts in the previous mix, brought about not by large-scale decisions but by small continuous adjustments, so that in various countries change is mainly incremental and adaptive.

Second, state and market are not the only two forms of regulation that warrant examination in the economic sphere. Alongside them, communitarian regulation has continued to perform a significant function, and associational regulation is becoming increasingly important. Where communitarian institutions predominate, the co-ordination of activities and the allocation of resources take place mainly through forms of spontaneous solidarity. This solidarity may stem from norms, customs or values shared by the members of the community (whether this is a family, clan, subculture or social movement) and may be based on respect, trust and so forth. Or it may derive from simple identification with the community and therefore with its rules and hierarchies. Belonging to a community depends, in fact, on either ascriptive criteria or on processes which create 'collective identities' (Pizzorno 1978). Nevertheless, in many communities, both authority relationships and exchange relationships perform the important function of strengthening normative bonds, and the latter are difficult to understand without taking account of the former.

With regard to associational regulation, it has been observed that an increasing number of economic activities are regulated by 'the public use of private organized interests' (Streeck and Schmitter 1985) – that is, by agreements among a few large-scale interest associations which hold monopoly (or at least oligopoly) over the representation of functionally defined interests, high disruptive power regarding each other's activities and the maintenance of the social order, and which consequently gain priority recognition from other associations and the public authorities. Unlike the contracts typical of market relationships, these concerted agreements generally presuppose a long-term strategic capacity which enables actors to underutilize their market power and, in general, their disruptive power. These agreements often require the exercise of legitimate authority for their enforcement, as well as the direct or implicit co-operation of the state, if they are to be successful. This is because they usually involve the devolution of public functions to the private organizations participating in the concertation and the assignment to these of state resources in order to offset the costs or risks of their participation. These agreements may be rendered highly unstable by the emergence of internal crises of representation. For this reason, their success depends largely on the associations' exercise of hierarchical control over their members and on the ability of the former to provide 'identity incentives' – ones based on shared values – for the latter (Regini 1981).

Third, mention should be made of the increasing importance of levels other than the centralized or macro-national one – that is, the level at which the phenomena traditionally studied by political economy lie. The Keynesian regulation of the economy, the participation of organized interests in social concertation, the growth of the welfare state (i.e., the phenomena studied in Part I) – these are macro-phenomena which lie principally at the centralized national level. However, over the past fifteen years or so, certain functions of economic regulation have been taken over by both subnational and supranational institutions. Moreover, events at the micro-level of the firm – that is, in the institutions and inter-actor relationships that manage economic adjustment (which is the subject of Part II) – appear much more closely tied to trends which occur at the macro-level and closely condition them.

Perception of this latter phenomenon has led to a revision of the political lexicon: the terms 'welfare state', 'Keynesianism' and 'neocorporatism' have been progressively replaced by 'flexibility', 'deregulation' and 'micro-corporatism'. This, however, is not just a change of vocabulary or of conceptual apparatus brought about by the dictates of fashion. The first group of concepts, in fact, relate to those models of concerted and centralized political management of the capitalist economy and of its potential crises which today have apparently lost their significance. The second group of concepts encapsulate tendencies towards economic adjustment based on micro-social mechanisms of regulation, tendencies which in recent years have forcefully asserted themselves – in some cases in antithesis to the former ones, in others at any rate conditioning the direction of their development.

We must therefore also examine what may be called the peripheral or local mechanisms that regulate the economy. Above all, we must analyse those trends at the micro-level of the firm and of production which exert a potentially major impact on trends at the macro-level. Such analysis, long considered extraneous to the paradigm of political economy, has only recently, and only partially, become an integral part of it. Although important steps forward have been taken with regard to the former aspect – that is, the social and political institutions which regulate the economy at the local or peripheral level (Trigilia 1986; Bagnasco 1988; Sabel 1989) – there is still a great deal to be done with regard to the latter – that is, the micro/macro relationship which constitutes the major theme of this book. However, there is no doubt that, for example, the future of redistributive mechanisms like the welfare state or opportunities for the concertation of economic policies closely depend on – and in turn influence – changes taking place in organizational patterns and institutional arrangements at the level of production. Unless this integration between micro and macro is vigorously pursued, the paradigm of political economy which has so long been of major importance in study of the relationships between economy and society risks impoverishment, and it may lose all its capacity to give a thorough account of contemporary reality.

Comment must still be made concerning the value options that colour many studies of the relationships between economy and society. Several accounts from a political economy perspective, particularly those most widespread during the 1970s and early 1980s, exhibit a clear metascientific bias towards the 'Keynesian welfare state plus concertation' model which for many years dominated debate within the international Left and the experience of various European countries. For those in the advanced industrial countries who inquired into the conditions for a programme of major reforms, many of the phenomena studied by political economy appeared important because they were the ingredients of the class compromise which in its most advanced form became concrete in the 'Swedish model'. These ingredients were, of course,

the following: Keynesianism as an instrument for the political management of
the capitalist economy; the welfare state and full employment as redistributive
mechanisms and guarantors of consensus; neocorporatism as the institutional
arrangement of consensual relationships between government and organized
interests; and social democracy as the overall political and ideological setting.
The implicit aim of analysing these topics was to understand the conditions
under which they had become established in certain countries and the extent to
which they could be reproduced in others.

Now that this hegemonic model is in crisis, and now that the utopia of
major reforms has given way to a more pragmatic approach, study of the
shifting boundaries and mutable interrelations between state, market and other
forms of social regulation has lost its appeal. Furthermore, because the decline of the hegemonic model has led to growing differences among countries
and regions, the task has become more difficult. It is now necessary, in fact, to
uncover partial patterns rather than to draw sweeping generalizations.

Yet discovering these patterns in the new boundaries and interrelations now
emerging is perhaps an even more urgent task, an intellectual challenge that
cannot be ignored. Phenomena no less important than those relating to the
conditions of the Keynesian welfare state must be studied: how a particular
mix of different regulatory institutions works; how this mix changes (rarely
univocally and abruptly, more often with slight but constant internal shifts);
what roles may be assumed today by the state regulation of the economy;
whether the revival of the market, as well as of features of traditional society,
may not exacerbate dualisms and discontinuities (Berger and Piore 1980)
rather than represent a simple reversal of previous trends. Finally, one must
establish whether the forms of micro-social regulation that made the economic
adjustment of the 1980s possible are a viable alternative to the centralized
political regulation of the economy, and whether the substantial co-operation
that accompanied them can replace the consensus once reached through
macro-national concertation, or whether, instead, new equilibria between
micro and macro must be sought.

On these and other topics, research is only beginning, research to which
this book endeavours to make a modest, but one would hope useful, contribution.

PART I

The rise and decline of the political regulation of the economy

In contemporary Western economies, the principal institution regulating economic activities is the market. According to the traditional view, the liberal state should refrain from intervening in the economy. Consequently, a sharp distinction should be drawn between the tasks and spheres of action pertaining to the market (chief institution of the economic system) and those pertaining to the state (the paramount institution of the political system). Nevertheless, the history of this century has been marked by constant shifts, spillovers and blurring of this traditional distinction, mainly because of two enduring phenomena.

On the one hand, increasing intervention by the state in the economy (which I examine in Chapter 1) has led to a marked expansion of political regulation and a corresponding decline in regulation by the market, an expansion which has only recently come to a halt, to differing extents in different countries. On the other, there has been a manifest tendency for the distribution of the resources produced or allocated by the state to take place according to criteria of exchange and private appropriation, and not according to administrative rationality geared to the public interest. The development of large interest organizations and political exchange (which I examine in Chapters 2 and 3) is an integral part of this process.

This redrawing of the boundaries between economy, politics and society has to some extent been the unintended outcome of multiple small shifts in the roles traditionally performed by state, market and organized social interests. To a larger extent, however, it has derived from an institutional design which we may call the 'concerted and centralized political regulation' of the market economies. This is a model of regulation which assigns to the state and to large interest organizations – or, better, to their institutional and organizational bodies operating at the centre, not the periphery, of the economy – crucial tasks in the allocation of resources, the aim being to counteract certain socially undesirable outcomes of the workings of the market. These tasks consist mainly in restoring balanced economic growth and in providing partial compensation for the inequalities of income and power that the market generates.

Having defined the model of concerted and centralized political regulation in these terms, we may now begin a broad analysis of the first of its features: namely, increasing state intervention in the industrialized economies since the 1930s – in the years after the Second World War in particular – and its crisis during the 1980s.

1

The Keynesian welfare state and its crisis

This chapter concentrates on the roughly fifty-year period from the mid-1930s to the early 1980s. This is not to imply, however, that before this period the state performed no function in the market economies.

THE TRADITIONAL ECONOMIC FUNCTIONS OF THE STATE

Economic historians have identified three major traditional functions of the state – functions performed even during the phase of the so-called liberal state which adhered to the doctrines of laissez-faire – in capitalist systems. The first of these is the creation and enforcement of a legal code which guarantees and reproduces existing relations of production and which makes exchange possible. The right to private ownership, the enforcement of contracts, the regulation of free competition – without these legal institutions the free market as we know it today could not have developed.

The second traditional function of the state is to manage international economic relationships in such a way that national capital is defended and augmented on world markets. Historically, such management has taken forms ranging from the aggressive behaviour associated with colonialism and imperialism to others more defensive in character, such as protectionism and currency devaluation, in order to enhance the competitiveness of the country's products.

The third function is to guarantee the 'material conditions of production', that is, the supply of at least some of the inputs that the productive process needs: labour, capital, technology and infrastructures. Although the importance of each of these inputs has varied from one period to another, the role of the state, in its various forms, has almost invariably been decisive in ensuring their supply. With regard to the labour force, one need only cite the function performed by legislation in ensuring a quantitatively and qualitatively adequate supply of labour (from the early English enclosures, to the laws regulating migratory flows, to the public provision of education and vocational training). Regarding the provision of capital, the state has played a decisive role in the industrial take-off of some latecomer countries (Gerschenkron 1962) and has continued to perform an important function in various countries by extending the public sector of the economy. The technology necessary for economic development has also often been supplied by the state, either indirectly (e.g., through warfare or space programmes) or directly (by means of public research programmes). And the creation of the many infrastructures equally indispensable to this development (railways, motorways, electrical power, etc.) could hardly have been possible, in many countries, without the state's direct intervention.

These, then, have been the state's functions in facilitating development. But one can assert, following Polanyi (1944), that the organization itself of economic systems based on the market, as the chief resource-allocating mechanism, has historically had to be imposed by the state in order to overcome the antimarket resistances raised by pre-established interests.

Finally, if we shift our attention away from the state's historical role as the regulator and facilitator of economic development and concentrate instead on its redistributive action – that is, on its function as an allocator of economic resources implicit in social policies – it is equally evident that this phenomenon is not unique to the past fifty years. Indeed, the numerous comparative studies of the development of the welfare state (see, e.g., Flora and Heidenheimer 1981; Alber 1982) show that its first stage of growth lasted from midway through the nineteenth century until the Second World War. Initially, some European governments were concerned simply to counteract, to some extent and with ad hoc measures, the excessive impoverishment of the urban proletariat caused by extensive industrialization, as well as to repair the grave damage wreaked by war.

However, with Bismarck's introduction of compulsory social insurance for industrial wage-earners in 1883–9, the principal function of social policy became that of backing up the operation of the labour market. This was certainly not a conception of the welfare state as the universal right of all citizens to certain minimum standards of living; it was instead a social security measure aimed solely at those operating in the labour market, assisting them when they were temporarily unable to work or when they retired. When workers fully participated in the labour market, however, they were left to the free play of its forces – with which there was certainly no intention to interfere. In accordance with the doctrine of the liberal state, intervention by the state was purely ancillary to the workings of the market. It was an emergency measure designed to restore the system of the satisfaction of needs – which was normally based on other institutions (the market, the family, community networks) – when these failed to function properly (Balbo 1987). Thus, far from obstructing the market, in this period the welfare state sustained it, by ensuring what neo-Marxist analyses would call the 'social reproduction of the labour force' (Lenhardt and Offe 1977).

But if the state had always fulfilled certain functions in support of economic development, one may ask why, from the 1930s in Sweden and in the United States of the New Deal onwards, and after the Second World War in several European countries, did a profound change (and not just simple growth) occur in the state's role vis-à-vis the economy? Why, with reference to the New Deal and Keynesian doctrines, do scholars contrast the antecedent liberal state with the advent of an 'interventionist state'? And why do students of the welfare state regard the Beveridge Report of 1942 as a true turning-point, as the beginning of the social state as we know it today? What new functions crucial to the workings of the economy did the state perform during the fifty years or so in question? To what structural changes in the operation of economic and political systems are these new functions connected, and what consequences and new contradictions have they generated?

These questions have received different answers in the literature. Some of them are more precise because they are couched in the technical language of public finance and economic policy (although for this reason they are somewhat reductive). Others, those furnished by political science and political economy, are more suggestive and thought-provoking – though often less rigorous – because they assign a decisive role to political factors and actors' strategies. In the following sections of this chapter I shall summarize as clearly as possible the answers of this latter type. Although it is by now difficult to add anything new to the many analyses available, I shall propose a re-reading of the adoption of Keynesian policies and the development of the welfare state not as two separate phenomena largely stemming from particular techniques of government, but as essential components of a model of economic regulation aimed at specific goals, based on specific instruments and dense with more or less expected consequences – the model that I earlier called 'concerted and centralized political regulation'.

From this point of view, the state decisively changes its role in the economic system when it assumes two crucial functions besides the traditional ones described earlier. The first of them we may call 'control of the economic cycle and of crises', where the aim is to stabilize the cyclical trend of capitalist development caused by a lack of overall co-ordination, thereby avoiding repetition of the disastrous crises that have marked such development and their consequences: the destruction of socially accumulated wealth and social revolt. This was the manifest objective of Keynesian doctrines and the various public policies they inspired (Skidelsky 1979; Bordogna and Provasi 1984).

The second function (which, as we shall see, is closely linked with the first) we may call the 'control of consensus': the securing of mass consensus for the economic and political systems of the advanced capitalist democracies, mainly through the diffusion of social services, the guarantee of full employment and the maintenance of surplus population, that is, through the welfare state in its most fully developed form (O'Connor 1973). Of course, the assurance of social order is the traditional political function of every state, but from various points of views, in this period it became an economic function as well, as we shall see.

THE DEVELOPMENT OF THE KEYNESIAN WELFARE STATE

Why, since the 1930s, has the goal of stabilizing the cyclical trend of capitalist development and averting its disastrous consequences become of such central importance? It is possible to show that international capitalist development has always followed a cyclical pattern of rapid expansion followed by stagnation or recession. Although long-term trends emphasize development, cyclical oscillations internal to them have generated profound crises, which in some cases have jeopardized the stability of the economic system that produced them.

Economists have always assigned a place of paramount importance in their theories to the economic cycle. For neoclassical economists, the cycle is a physiological phenomenon, in that every period of recession serves to re-create the bases for greater accumulation in the period that follows, forcing marginal firms out of the market and encouraging industrial concentration and efficiency. For Marxist economists, the recurrent crises produced by the cyclical trend manifest the fundamental contradictions of the capitalist mode of production, which is able to achieve development only at the price of the large-scale destruction of socially accumulated wealth, with the unemployment and impoverishment of the masses that this entails. For both schools of thought, however, the source of this cyclical trend and its inevitable attendant crises is 'the anarchy of the market' – as the Marxists used to term it – or the 'decentralization of economic decisions at the level of individual market participants, without any overall co-ordination', to use the expression of liberal economists and political scientists (e.g., Lindblom 1977). The sum of these individual uncoordinated decisions may produce aggregate consequences which no individual subject is able to control, even less able to direct. The 'invisible hand' of the market, which has generated the West's extraordinary development over the past two or three centuries, is therefore also responsible for the most grievous episodes of crisis, impoverishment and potential social disorder.

One of the severest of these crises, the Great Crash of 1929, shook not only the economic certitudes of the West but also its social stability. The idea thus arose – to be developed theoretically by Keynes (1936), whose doctrines spread rapidly through the Anglo-Saxon world (Weir 1987) and were proved politically practicable by Roosevelt's New Deal – that the state could intervene to combat the anarchy of the market, to stabilize the cycle and to prevent crises from recurring. With what instruments? Keynesian doctrine recommended mainly fiscal policy instruments, whereas the neo-Keynesians later insisted on others, chiefly incomes policies (which lie at the heart of the concertation practices described in the next chapter). Here, however, my concern is less to describe the technical devices of state intervention than to identify the preconditions and consequences of what some have called a historical compromise between state and market, but which was certainly also a class compromise corresponding to a particular phase of history (Korpi 1983; Bordogna and Provasi 1984; Przeworski 1985; Goldthorpe 1987).

There is, however, an instrument – indeed, it is the chief instrument of classical Keynesian policies – which warrants brief examination because it is closely linked with some of the 'perverse effects' that subsequently made their appearance. I refer to public spending. In simple and necessarily reductive terms, the basic idea was this: the state could utilize its spending power, and indeed spend more than its revenues would permit (deficit spending), to increase demand for market goods to a greater or lesser extent depending on the phase of the cycle, thereby acting as the overall regulator of aggregate demand. In theory, the state could thus 'damp' the economy in boom periods in order to counteract inflationary tendencies, and it could, above all (because this was the problem then deemed crucial), impede the classical crises of overproduction and underconsumption and ensure the full employment of all the production factors, chief among which was labour.

In order to do this, the state institutions had two principal strategies available. First, they could use public spending to purchase goods in the private sector of the economy. This would probably induce employment to grow in order to meet the increase in demand; or employers would increase overtime; or, again, employers would try to increase productivity and offer higher wages in return. In any case, the aggregate capacity for consumption by workers in the private sector would increase, and this would in turn engender greater demand for market goods. Alternatively, rather than purchase goods, the government could decide to increase public-sector employment (or to extend public welfare). This strategy, too, would lead both to an increase in employment levels and to greater aggregate consumption, with the same effects as already mentioned. In all cases, the growth of both aggregate wages and profits should have the further effect of expanding the tax base (and thereby rebalancing the state budget) while at the same time triggering a virtuous circle of development. The first important experiment of this kind, Roosevelt's New Deal, in fact combined three major public programmes: an expansion of the social services (the educational system in particular), a broad programme of public works and an extension of public welfare programmes (Piven and Cloward 1971; Skocpol and Ikenberry 1985).

After the Second World War, this particular compromise between state and market spread, albeit to various extents, to almost all Western countries – not just because it was an instrument with which to co-ordinate the economy and avert cyclical crises, but because the governing élites saw it as the most reliable means with which to secure the consensus of the subordinate classes. In other words, the need to stabilize the economic cycle is not enough to explain the enormous growth of public intervention in the economy after the Second World War (Rose 1984). Keynesian policies also proved a valuable instrument – justified on the basis of economic goals – with which to satisfy a specifically political requirement of the democracies reborn or revitalized after the war: namely, that of winning mass consensus for the new regimes.

Popular participation in the political process required new instruments of consensus. The conviction spread that the stability of the new democratic regimes depended on the ability of the state to provide its citizens with services that satisfied their principal social needs and to redistribute by political means, to a certain extent, the wealth unequally allocated by the operation of market mechanisms. Most of the dominant political élites – certainly the social democratic ones, but also those of the Catholic countries – firmly believed that the market was the economic institution that could most efficiently promote development; but also that it produced such severe inequalities in distribution that the survival itself of those not active in the labour market was threatened. For this reason, public spending often extended well beyond the Keynesian imperatives of macroeconomic management, and it was principally directed towards social goals (almost everywhere social spending accounted for an increasing percentage of total public spending): the achievement of full employment, the building of a system of social services as the right of all citizens, and not just of certain categories, public welfare programmes for those excluded from the labour market.

This was the promise of the new development phase of the welfare state described by the Beveridge Report of 1942 and then implemented, to various extents and in various forms, in many countries. The essential difference with respect to the previous phase was the universalization of social welfare provision so that it encompassed all citizens. In the new conception of the welfare state – or, better, in its 'institutional/redistributive' version (Titmuss 1974) – there was no room for selectivity in public intervention. The welfare state became the right of every citizen to enjoy certain guaranteed minimum standards of living – in health, housing, education and so on (Bendix 1964).

These social objectives have constituted some of the basic goals of labour movements (European ones at least) ever since their creation. Job and income security for all workers has always been of paramount importance, both for a working class subject to the iron laws of the capitalist labour market and for its representative organizations, which draw their power from their ability to guarantee such security. In order to achieve these goals, labour movements first created solidaristic institutions and then exerted pressure on the state (sometimes on individual firms).

But these social objectives also became increasingly central to government action (at least until 1980s) in almost all the industrialized countries. The social legislation enacted in various countries merged, as we have seen, with the adoption of Keynesian economic policies to produce an unprecedented expansion of expenditure on social security. According to the detailed list drawn up by Wilensky (1975: 2–3), in the advanced industrialized countries this expenditure included

three expensive programs: pensions, death benefits, disability insurance; sickness and/or maternity benefits or health insurance or a national health service like Britain's; and family or child allowances. Also included are the less expensive programs of workmen's compensation or work-injury protection, unemployment compensation, and related labor market policies; 'public assistance' or 'social assistance' including miscellaneous aid to the handicapped and the poor; and benefits for war victims.

Social security policies thus became a key concern not only for the strategy of labour movements, but for state intervention in the economic system as well. In the 1970s, together with incomes and industrial policies, these social security policies were also the focus of the relationships between governments and organized interests that I analyse in the next chapter.

After the Second World War, therefore, the welfare state developed much more rapidly than before. What, beyond the generic need for consensus mentioned earlier, were the factors responsible for the development? Various theories have been put forward by sociologists and political scientists to account for it.

The by now classic analyses of Marshall (1964) and Bendix (1964) view the rise of the welfare state as the natural extension of universal rights of citizenship from the realm of civil and political rights to that of 'social rights'. Because of their emphasis on élite values and ideas in this process, and because of their evolutionist and unilinear account of this expansion, these analyses can be criticized for their overly ideological bias. Above all, they seem unable to account for the numerous contradictions and gaps in the process – shortcomings which are also partly present in those other analyses (although based on historical documentation) that tie the evolution of the welfare state to the processes of industrialization and modernization (Rimlinger 1971; Heclo 1974; Flora and Heidenheimer 1981; Flora 1986).

Other students of the rise of the welfare state have dispensed with the traditional historical-comparative approach and have preferred instead to conduct quantitative analyses based on comparisons among national statistics and measuring the influence of various variables. Wilensky (1975), for instance, explores the causal links between the percentage of social expenditure in the GDP of each country and such variables as its rate of economic growth, the age of its social security system, the degree of centralization of its political system and its population structure. Apart from the almost inevitable crudity of the indicators used to measure some of these variables, analysis of this kind reveals only whether or not the development of the welfare state is associated with these phenomena. It is unable to furnish a model which explains this development; even less can it account for the differing forms that development has taken in various countries or historical periods, beyond providing the purely quantitative measure of public spending for social purposes.

Other theories, notably neo-Marxist accounts of the role of the state (O'Connor 1973; Offe 1984), as well as a number of national case studies belonging to the same school of thought (e.g., Piven and Cloward 1971, on the U.S. case), offer an explanation based on the distinction and possible contradiction between two functions of the state: accumulation and legitimation. These theories claim that the development of social services and most social security programmes has been due to the state's obligation to sustain capital accumulation. The function of this type of public spending ('social consumption' in O'Connor's terminology) is to socialize the costs of labour reproduction, and it is therefore indirectly productive. In contrast, social security programmes which are not even indirectly productive (what O'Connor calls 'social expense of production') owe their development to the state's need for legitimation. The state redistributes some of the material resources produced by capitalist development to groups harmed by or excluded from this development in order to ensure their loyalty. The greater or lesser development of the welfare state therefore depends on the ways in which the two requirements of accumulation and legitimation take material form (and possibly contradict each other).

Although this theory is more sophisticated than the others, it suffers from the typical functionalist weakness of explaining the development of the welfare state in terms of its functions or dysfunctions. It is not clear which subjects act to fulfil the 'needs of the system' (needs which social spending is supposed to satisfy), by means of which actions and processes or with what results. On this account, a sociologically indeterminate actor, namely the state, is taken to be the only subject of conscious action designed either to promote accumulation or to secure consensus.

By contrast, what has been called the 'social democratic model of the welfare state'(Shalev 1983) seeks to explain the level and form of its development on the basis of the political and market power exerted by national labour movements, of the relationships between their political wing and the trade unions and of the role of the welfare state in their strategy. This model therefore scales down the contribution made to the development of the welfare state by far-sighted and enlightened élites seeking to enlarge the base of their political consensus. Instead, it sees this development as essentially the outcome of class politics prosecuted by labour movements attempting to shift the distributional conflict from the market to the political arena (Korpi 1983; Esping-Andersen 1985).

This account, too, is highly partial and unable to provide a thorough explanation of the differing extents to which the welfare state has developed in various countries (for a critical approach from within this theory, see Shalev 1983). Nevertheless, it at least has the merit of being based on concrete actors, with their own interests, their own levels of relative power and their own strategies. The need for social consensus as already outlined only constitutes the context that renders feasible and, in the end, successful the strategies of the actors who endeavour to satisfy it. It is not this context that yields actors, strategies and behaviours, however, but the operation of other systems (the economic system, the political-institutional system and the system of interest representation). Only by examining these, therefore, can one understand why similar needs for consensus in diverse countries and periods have produced different social policies.

This type of analysis is conducted in Chapter 3, to which the reader is referred. As specifically regards the welfare state, it is precisely because actors – public institutions and organized interests – possess specific characteristics, strategies and forms of interaction that the features of the social security system of one country differ from those of another. Of these distinctive features, the following seem to be particularly important.

1. *The structure of the welfare system.* This is defined by the relative positions (central or marginal) of each specific welfare institution or programme – old-age pensions, unemployment benefits, health insurance and so on – within the overall system. Even on cursory examination, in fact, different welfare systems display differing arrangements of similar institutions and programmes. For example, public assistance in Italy has developed to a lesser

extent than it has in other countries, whereas the reverse is true of social insurance. Or again, Italy has given much greater priority to measures combatting disguised unemployment among the already employed (the Cassa Integrazione Guadagni, Wages Guarantee Fund) than it has to unemployment benefits in general.

2. *The extent of the protection provided by welfare institutions.* Social security programmes may be aimed only at subjects active in the labour market (or only at certain categories of them) or at larger groups. In this respect, too, welfare systems vary considerably.

3. *The degree of equality among the services and benefits delivered to welfare programme recipients.* In fact, the amount and quality of the welfare services provided are not necessarily uniform for all categories of citizens entitled to receive them. The criteria determining those eligible to benefit from higher levels of service differ from one system to another.

4. *The management and administration of welfare programmes.* The representatives of those directly affected by the development of a social policy may be involved to various extents in its management. Representatives of political parties, unions and employers' associations frequently participate – with different responsibilities – in the administration of welfare programmes or their funds, in some cases flanked by representatives of their users.

Although not specifically constructed on all four of these characteristics, a variety of 'types' of welfare state have been proposed as a basis for empirical inquiry (see Titmuss 1974 for the basic typology out of which subsequent models have evolved). However, I will not discuss the relative merits and shortcomings of these types here. I shall instead restrict myself to describing the development of the welfare state in Italy as a concrete example of a hybrid among analytically distinct types (see the first section of Chapter 4).

PERVERSE EFFECTS AND RESPONSES TO THE CRISIS

The growth of the Keynesian welfare state brought with it a number of unintended and to some extent perverse effects – effects which have been responsible for the crisis in this mode of regulating the economy during the past two decades and which have also produced diverse attempts to cope with it. Certain exogenous factors – the international inflation caused by the financing of the Vietnam War by the United States, for instance, or the oil shocks of the 1970s – which worsened the performance of the Western economies, also helped to trigger the crisis in the state's regulatory and distributive functions. Nevertheless, there is no doubt that the most severe difficulties stemmed from endogenous factors closely connected to the form that the Keynesian welfare state came to assume in the course of its development.

The first two unintended consequences of this development relate to the goals that the Keynesian welfare state explicitly set out to achieve: full employment and the reduction of social insecurity. It was, in fact, the substantial achievement of these two goals that provoked those unintended consequences, or contradictions, which eventually undermined the entire edifice of public intervention. As Kalecki (1943) had predicted, the quasi-full employment which, by the mid-1960s, characterized almost all the advanced industrial democracies led to a sharp increase in the market power of workers. This in turn strengthened their bargaining power: a situation which in some countries – in combination with other conditions, as in Italy – bred generalized industrial conflict and social mobilization, while in others it increased wage pressures and thereby exacerbated the inflation already set in train by other causes (Soskice 1978). Full employment induced politically – not induced, that is, by the 'natural' workings of the market – thus became one of the chief targets of criticism by conservative forces during the 1970s and an objective which even left-wing European governments found increasingly difficult to pursue, with the exception of Sweden (Scharpf 1984).

Reducing social insecurity was a goal implicit in the conception of the welfare state as the protection provided for the individual and his or her primary social needs against the ruthless operation of the market. However, as Polanyi (1944) had already pointed out in his description of the historic episode of Speenhamland, state protection against market mechanisms may slacken the incentive to work. And it was this awareness that Piven and Cloward (1971) assumed to be the principal reason for the (scant) development of social policies in the United States. In extremely generous and highly developed welfare states like those of Scandinavia, lesser social insecurity may eventually lead to the almost complete uncoupling of life-chances from the market (Offe 1984), the outright 'de-commodification of the labour force' (Esping-Andersen 1987). It is therefore evident why this aspect, too, was targeted by the political coalitions that conducted the most aggressive critique against the Keynesian welfare state.

As well as its declared and substantially achieved objectives, however, the instruments used by the welfare state generated perverse effects over the years. Consider one of the chief instruments of Keynesian policies, whose 'virtuous circle' effects were discussed in the preceding section: public spending to counteract the economic cycle. The Keynesian model of state intervention was, so to speak, abstractly symmetrical. It envisaged the injection of a greater amount of public spending into the market in order to sustain aggregate demand during recessionary phases and lesser amounts during boom periods in order to contain inflation. This image of policy-making probably corresponded, in Keynes and among his followers, to the utopia of a government of experts, one which restricted its action to adjusting macroeconomic variables without being obliged to respond to social and political pressures (Skidelsky 1979). One realizes immediately, however, that this is indeed a utopia. Whereas governments find it easy to gain consensus for a spending programme, they encounter much greater difficulty in building social and political coalitions around programmes which entail reductions or substantial cutbacks in the budget.

Experience in Britain (the Thatcher government) and the United States (the Reagan administration) shows that it is extremely difficult to implement reductions in public spending, even when the government has decided or seriously intends to pursue this policy (Hall 1986). In fact, examination of social spending (in all countries) over recent decades reveals its extraordinary downward rigidity. Although this has not yet produced a 'fiscal crisis of the state' as grave as was predicted in the 1970s (O'Connor 1973), it thwarts the use of public spending as an anticyclical device.

These perverse effects of the expansion of the Keynesian welfare state are undeniable, and they have been largely responsible for government élites' and interest organizations' increasing disaffection with – if not outright hostility towards – this model of economic regulation and resource allocation by political means. Nevertheless, neither political nor scientific debate has yet been able to come up with attractive and viable alternatives. Indeed, some commentators (Goldthorpe 1987) have argued that the two principal alternatives suggested to date – the 'neo-laissez-faire' and 'neo-interventionist' options – encounter obstacles just as insurmountable as those that obstructed the progress of the Keynesian welfare state. Can some satisfactory way out of the dilemma be discerned in current analyses of the crisis of the Keynesian welfare state?

To begin with, what is the concrete significance of the welfare state and its crisis for citizens? For many of them, it means (almost) free access to services (health, education, etc.) which would otherwise be extremely costly, but at the same time awareness of the progressive deterioration in the quality of such services. For some, it means an income which substitutes for earnings from work (pension, unemployment benefit, etc.), albeit an income which is often inadequate to meet their needs and which falls short of the price paid by individuals and the collectivity. For others, it means entry into the hidden economy – with its employment opportunities and social costs – made possible by the minimum level of subsistence guaranteed by the state (early retirement pensions and free health care).

People may therefore often be disappointed by the welfare state, but they cannot do without it in the absence of credible and viable alternatives. This is the origin of many of the problems, ambiguities and uncertainties that have marked responses to its crisis. Of course, there is the awareness that what has been depicted as the 'welfare' state entails considerable social costs: often excessive levels of public spending, a heavy tax burden, dissatisfaction among the users of welfare services, dysfunctions in the labour market. But how can these disadvantages be eliminated without reneging on the promises of full employment and guaranteed protection against social evils that have always constituted the welfare state's historical rationale?

Neo-laissez-faire thinkers believe that theirs is a simple prescription because the analysis upon which it rests is simple. Echoing some of the arguments just discussed, they contend that the achievement of full employment and guaranteed social benefits stunts the incentive to work, and this prevents the market from functioning properly. The uncontrolled expansion of the protected public sector restricts opportunities for investment in the private sector. Finally, the vision of the welfare state as a right of citizenship constantly stimulates demand for further state welfare provision, thereby provoking fiscal crisis and ungovernability. The neo-laissez-faire remedy for these problems is to set curbs on public spending, to privatize social services and to allow the free operation of market forces. Nevertheless, even if we grant that this prescription rests on an analysis which grasps important truths, it encounters obstacles, resistances and political constraints that restrict its viability even in the countries that have been most determined to implement it – Margaret Thatcher's Britain, for instance, or Ronald Reagan's United States.

On the other hand, among the European social democracies – where the welfare state has always been the cornerstone of social programmes – one discerns uncertainties and differences stemming from the different histories of these countries.

For the Scandinavian countries especially, the contemporary welfare state is the outcome of political strategy and culture. The strains to which Scandinavian welfare states are now subject derive not from their faulty operation, but from the improper functions that the economy and labour market have obliged them to perform. Under the social democratic governments, Keynesian economic policy pursued the goal of full employment, of the absorption of the labour supply into productive activity. Social security programmes were devised for those members of the population excluded from the labour market, even in a full-employment economy, because they were old, sick, handicapped or temporarily unemployed.

The social contributions and taxes paid by the employed could be used to develop services available to all citizens: primarily a public health service and educational programmes designed to deliver a better-trained labour supply to the productive system. State and market thus kept their spheres of action distinct and did not interfere with each other. Social or citizenship rights propagated the ideas of equality, solidarity and redistribution without encroaching on the rights of ownership and private enterprise. If, as many have written, this was a class compromise (Korpi 1983; Bordogna and Provasi 1984; Goldthorpe 1987), then entrusting the state with the task of guaranteeing social services and protection against the risks of the market by transforming it into a social state undoubtedly constituted the side to the compromise that favoured the workers.

It is only to be expected that neo-laissez-faire theorists should blame the dysfunctions of the economy on this compromise between politics and market. And it is equally natural that socialist currents in these countries should defend 'their' welfare state, blaming its crisis on the fact that increasingly serious distortions in the labour market are off-loaded onto the welfare state, which was conceived not as a remedy for the structural limits of capitalist development, but only as a buffer against secondary and contingent tensions. As Hinrichs et al. (1985: 416) have written: 'It is not the particular arrangements of the welfare state that have caused this crisis, but the societal institutions of the labour market and work contracts, of whose dynamic the crisis of the welfare state is only a reflection'.

The capacity of the labour market to absorb all those who depend on it because they do not have alternative work- and life-chances is clearly diminishing. We are then faced with a dilemma: the more welfare measures are needed to compensate for the fewer work opportunities provided by the economic system, the less these measures can be relied upon to solve the problem, given that their financial resources depend precisely on the good performance of the economy and the labour market. Therefore, 'if the crisis [of the welfare state] must be resolved, it can only be so from outside the welfare state itself; that is, at the level of those societal institutions on which it is dependent' (Hinrichs et al. 1985: 416).

From this perspective, therefore, it is a matter not of changing the welfare system, but of counteracting the tendency of companies to increase productivity by shedding labour and off-loading costs onto the state. This tendency, which some years ago O'Connor (1973) was already citing as the cause of both the fiscal crisis of the state and the expansion of what today is called the informal economy, has intensified greatly in response to more severe international competition.

In fact, whereas from the point of view of the finances of the welfare state the optimum would obviously be an economy in which everyone works if they are able to, the optimal situation for the firm is one where the fewest workers produce the largest possible quantity of goods and services (Esping-Andersen 1986). But the welfare state programmes were originally designed to improve the conditions of only the elderly, the sick or the unemployed. These programmes were not intended to guarantee incomes for all the workers that companies wished to shed; nor to provide a core of guaranteed services and facilities which would enable these workers to leave the regular labour market and enter the hidden economy or self-employment; nor, finally, to enable workers in steady employment to resort to absenteeism for the purpose of moonlighting.

And yet, in the absence of full employment, the programmes of the welfare state do produce these perverse effects. Various research studies have shown that these programmes are widely exploited for the purposes just enumerated, even in those countries that have developed a welfare state as part of a wholly different social and political project. How are we to interpret, for example, the finding that 'in Germany 23% of people who are normally part of the work force, that is, those aged under 65, are active outside the labour market while they take advantage of the welfare state'? (Esping-Andersen 1986: 22). Certainly not as an increase in well-being among the working population, but rather as the improper use of early retirement to reduce the work force. Whatever the merits of this solution, it is enormously costly for the welfare state.

The improper use of the welfare state is not confined to companies, however. Workers, too, must often take the blame. We know that in countries where social rights have been developed to their fullest extent, there has been a major increase in idle work-time, with adverse effects on the state budget. In the Scandinavian countries, 'thanks to social rights, every day an average of around 10% of the labour force is absent from work, either because of illness or for maternity leave, or to attend training courses, or for some other reason' (Esping-Andersen 1986: 21). However one may judge this process of 'decommodification of the work force', the opinion widely held today is that the welfare state should not be called upon to pay for it.

For the European social democracies, therefore, the crucial answer is not to reduce the social benefits provided by the state; nor is it to improve the quality and efficiency of social services. The key courses of action, they believe, are to reform the labour market and the employment relationship so that job opportunities are redistributed among a greater proportion of the population, full employment is restored and the quality of work is enhanced. If this approach prevails, the future of the welfare state may be less uncertain than that of the Keynesian policies with which it has been traditionally associated.

2

Unstable concertation

In the 1960s, the attention of analysts was drawn to the state's increasing intervention in the economic system – that is, to its intervention in a sphere of activities previously dominated almost entirely by the market (Shonfield 1965). However, it was only toward the mid-1970s that the full importance was grasped of what was, in a certain sense, the phenomenon in reverse – the other side of the coin, so to speak: the reduction of the state and its economic resources (public spending) to a market, to a system of exchanges among organized social groups. In other words, the realization grew that public intervention in the economy, and the partial restriction of the market's sphere of influence that this entailed, came about less through the use of the bureaucratic structures of the traditional state than through forms of exchange, of institutionalized bargaining between governments and the large interest organizations. On the one hand, as we saw in the preceding chapter, the state thus assumed a key institutional role in the management of the economy. On the other, its economic decisions in turn became the object of bargaining – that is, of exchanges with other subjects, just as happens in a market. These other subjects were the large interest organizations, which, in order to equip themselves to handle these new relationships, progressively transformed their structure and their strategies.

POLITICAL EXCHANGE AND CONCERTATION

This realization bred various new concepts, such as 'political exchange' and 'political market' (Pizzorno 1978), or 'neocorporatism' and 'concertation' (Schmitter 1974; Lehmbruch 1977), concepts which, albeit in different ways, sought to incorporate these phenomena into the model of centralized political regulation that was apparently predominant in the early 1970s. A 'political market' is one in which 'an actor (generally the government) which has goods to give is ready to trade them in exchange for social consensus with an actor who can threaten to withdraw that consensus (or, which is more or less the same, to endanger order) unless he receives the goods he needs' (Pizzorno 1978: 279). In this kind of market, therefore, a type of exchange comes about which differs from collective bargaining both because the power of threat (wielded by the workers' organizations) concerns the withdrawal of co-operation in maintaining the social order – and not simply the withdrawal of co-operation over production – and because the market power of those who exercise this threat depends not on the demand for labour but on the size of the social group. Like the economic market, moreover, the political market also has its equilibrium mechanisms and its sources of disequilibrium.

These concepts of political market and political exchange were probably regarded as heresy by the custodians of the traditional disciplinary boundaries between economics and political science, and as a provocation by those who confined the action of the market and the principle of exchange to the economic system and who conceived the political system as structured solely by the authority of a state acting according to hierarchical-bureaucratic criteria. Nevertheless, they rapidly entered scientific and political debate because they encapsulated a set of phenomena which, although they had become increasingly important in the advanced industrial democracies, had not received the emphasis they warranted in descriptions of the relationship between society, politics and the economy since adequate conceptualization of them was lacking.

The first of these phenomena was already evident in the 1960s and was closely bound up with the development of the Keynesian welfare state analysed in the preceding chapter. The fact that, as a consequence of this development, the state had become a prime allocator of economic resources induced the more powerful actors – who had initially organized themselves in the economic system so that they could share in the distribution of the outcomes of the market's operation – to exploit their power and to gear their action increasingly towards conditioning the policies of the state. In other words, organized interests, which had formed within the market in order to negotiate the allocation of economic resources, found it increasingly rewarding to apply this method of bargaining in their dealings with public institutions precisely because it was through these institutions that the economy was now regulated and an increasing number of benefits distributed.

The second phenomenon – which made its dramatic appearance towards the mid-1970s – was the economic crisis. This the political élites read, at least in part, as a crisis in that capacity to regulate the economy on which the growth of the Keynesian welfare state had been founded (Lindberg and Maier 1985). And it acted as a powerful stimulus for governments to seek the support of large interest organizations by having them participate in economic policy-making. Two purposes were served by this strategy. First, the élites could compensate for the legitimacy they had lost as the authorities responsible for the country's economic performance with the legitimation offered them by the major social interests. Second, they could utilize these organizations as a key instrument with which to combat the economic crisis, if they were willing to direct the variables under their control (wage dynamics, investment decisions, etc.) towards this common goal or general interest.

This brief outline of the phenomena underlying the extraordinary spread of the method of political exchange in the 1970s already indicates that its rise, and subsequent decline, should be viewed as resulting from the convergence of the interests of the actors concerned. It is only within a more articulated framework of the gains and losses accruing to each actor – which I describe in the next section – that both the development and the instability of this aspect of centralized political regulation can be understood. This preliminary discussion is nevertheless sufficient to show that political exchange is, in fact, the systematic exchange of resources between the state and large interest organizations. More specifically, it is a relationship based on these subjects' reciprocal attribution of different forms of political power. The state devolves a portion of its decision-making authority in economic policy matters to organized interests, who help to determine the outcomes of political decisions and thereby benefit from the distribution of public resources, both material and symbolic. In exchange, the interest organizations offer their indirect political power to the state, guaranteeing it consensus and deploying their resources to ensure the legitimation, efficiency and effectiveness of the state's action.

Two peculiar features of this kind of exchange should be stressed, for they help to explain both the difficulties involved in structuring relationships between the state and organized interests in this way and their instability. First, this type of exchange is unequal over time. Whereas for state institutions the benefits offered by organized interests – benefits which are principally legitimation and self-restraint in their market behaviour – have an immediate impact, the reverse is almost never the case. The resources that the state is able to offer to interest organizations – whether these are concessions in social policy, fiscal policy and so on, organizational advantages or increased power – are mostly long-term benefits, ones which can be enjoyed and appreciated by the members of these organizations only in the future. A temporally asymmetrical exchange of this kind requires a high degree of trust on both sides, and as we shall see later, it is particularly susceptible to crises of representation, that is, to breakdowns in the relationship between the interest organizations and those represented by them.

Second, the actors participating in the political exchange are able to exert only partial control over the implementation of their decisions. Governments can devise policies favourable to one or all of the organized interests involved in the exchange, but they cannot ensure that the public administration will implement them in ways that effectively match the original intention. For the reasons just mentioned, the interest organizations, for their part, have a varying but never total ability to guarantee that their members will comply with the decisions taken. Also from this point of view, therefore, the participants in the exchange can never be certain that they will actually obtain the benefits for which they made concessions. Hence, beyond the historically specific reasons for the failure of political exchange, these two features provide a structural explanation for the strains to which this relationship is subject, and they account for its fragility.

It was largely in order to eliminate this fragility that several European governments increased their efforts to institutionalize political exchange in the 1970s. The large interest organizations were offered recognition, monopoly of representation, privileged access to state resources and even the devolution to them of public functions (Schmitter 1974; Offe 1981). At the same time, channels for public policy-making were structured so that these organizations could participate in the exchange on a stable basis (Lehmbruch 1977). It was this type of institutionalization of political exchange that constituted the array of relationships and the mode of policy-making known as 'neocorporatism' and 'concertation'.[1]

The offer of institutional recognition, of monopoly (or oligopoly) over representation, of privileged access to state resources, which is the first aspect of the institutionalization process, transforms the input to policy-making – that is, the mechanisms whereby social demands are articulated and transmitted to the economic policy authorities. In fact, it leads inevitably to the concentration of social interests, which in a system of pluralistic pressure are necessarily dispersed (see Chapter 3). This concentration comes about either through the aggregation of interests previously organized individually, thereby creating encompassing organizations, or through the exclusion of some of them from the political process. In either case, concertation is a 'limited-player game', to which only certain large-scale interest organizations are admitted.

Their participation in public-policy formation through institutional channels of consultation or co-management can, on the other hand, transform the output of policy-making – that is, the content of the policies themselves. In fact, whereas negotiations conducted, or pressures applied, from outside the policy-making process in order to obtain benefits almost inevitably result in 'distributive' policies, the stable participation in policy-making institutions by large-scale organizations, which are thereby attributed public status, may lead to the predominance of 'regulatory' policies (see Lowi 1972 for this terminology), because it favours the internalization of systemic constraints and joint responsibility in the achievement of general interests (see the first section of Chapter 3 for a discussion of these mechanisms within a broader model which I call 'oligopolistic bargaining').

In the 1970s, the method of systematic political exchange and its institutionalization in concertation arrangements became widespread in Europe – to the point that many observers were convinced that this was a trend to which all the advanced industrial countries would have to adjust, provided that the institutional and organizational conditions for it existed. In other words, both in the neocorporatist literature and among a good many policy-makers, a bias spread (although it was almost never expressed explicitly) which can be summarized as follows. First, concertation was emerging as a system of policy-making which more effectively addressed the problems of the industrial democracies; indeed, the 'neocorporatist countries' were those that had achieved the best economic and political performances. Second, for this reason, other countries felt impelled to follow this path, or would soon do so. Third, for concertation to become solidly established, however, certain institutional, organizational and cultural conditions were necessary; these were not reproducible at will, and their absence accounted for the instability of concertation in many countries.

The first of these convictions may have stemmed from social democratic value options – that is, those favouring the orderly participation of labour organizations in policy-making. But it was given empirical confirmation by numerous comparative studies (based on quantitative indicators) of the impact of concertation on the economic performances of the advanced industrial countries (Cameron 1984; Lange and Garrett 1985). During the 1970s, in fact, it was the countries with high levels of neocorporatism, like Austria, Sweden, Norway, Switzerland and Germany, which appeared best able to cope with the various aspects of the economic crisis (inflation, recession, unemployment, a fall in industrial productivity, a balance-of-payments deficit). In actual fact, however, more in-depth qualitative analyses, such as that conducted by Scharpf (1984), revealed that each of these countries performed well on some of these indicators but not on others, depending on the strategic choices taken by its government.[2] Nevertheless, the overall impression remained, and was apparently confirmed by Schmitter's (1981) brilliant empirical demonstration, that although these countries were not necessarily those best equipped to deal with the economic crisis, they were nevertheless the ones which most successfully resolved problems of governability. This, therefore, strengthened the conviction that concertation was the method of regulating the economy best suited to the advanced industrial democracies. And analysts were apparently thus exempt from the obligation to examine the conditions under which the actors able to implement concertation on a permanent basis would find it in their interest to do so.

The second conviction can be explained in terms of the first. The relative success of the above-mentioned countries in combatting the problems that, to various extents, afflicted all the Western democracies prompted the political élites of other countries to copy their institutional arrangements. This conviction, too, seems to have been borne out by the events of the late 1970s. Three major European countries with traditionally noncorporatist policy-making systems sought to introduce social pacts which resembled the arrangements already in place in the successful countries: Great Britain had its 'social contract' of 1974–9; Italy introduced its 'negotiated laws' during the 'national solidarity' period of 1977–9 (Regini 1984); and Spain formulated a series of framework agreements, in some cases tripartite, in others bipartite, which were signed almost yearly after the 'Moncloa pacts' of 1977 had stabilized the new democratic regime (Pérez Diaz 1987; Ojeda Avilés 1990). It was not until the fall of the British Labour government and the rise of Mrs Thatcher that this conviction was dispelled.

Paradoxically, however, it was precisely this outcome which reinforced the third conviction: that it was the lack of suitable institutional and organizational conditions, certainly not the behaviour and self-interested calculations of the actors involved, which caused the instability or failure of concertation. Systems of relationships between the state and organized interests that differed from concertation were simply taken to be systems in which the prerequisites for concertation were lacking. Even those authors who insisted on the intrinsic instability of concertation (Panitch 1977; Sabel 1981; to some extent Offe 1981) attributed it principally to the fact that the interest organizations which participate in the concertation of economic policy are subject to the tensions inherent in all representation systems. We may say that they regarded instability as due to the 'imperfect' structure of certain partners to concerted policy-making, not to the fact that their objective interests lay elsewhere. In short, it was the structure of these actors, not their strategy, that rendered concertation unstable.

THE DEVELOPMENT AND INSTABILITY OF POLITICAL EXCHANGE

Why, one may ask, must it be taken for granted that all actors regard concerted economic policy-making as being in their interests, that they prefer consensus-based strategies? It is only in certain circumstances, in fact, that these yield benefits that outweigh the costs involved. Hence, if we are to understand both the expansion of political exchange and concertation, and their instability and decline, it is the actors' systems of variable convenience that we must examine.

The neocorporatist literature contains a good deal of analysis of government strategies, and it views the tendency to involve organized interests in the production of public policies as an attempt to deal with two main problems which – in terms of my discussion in the preceding chapter – were unintended effects of the Keynesian welfare state. The first of these problems was the 'excessive' bargaining power of labour, and in some cases its frequent recourse to industrial conflict, that ensued from the achievement of full employment. Where it was not possible to use authoritarian instruments to control the effects of such power, the most effective strategy available to governments was to shift the arena of distributional conflict from the market to the political system, where the trade unions' willingness to restrain themselves could be rewarded with benefits of another kind (welfare measures and political power).

The second problem was the proliferation of social interests which organized themselves to apply pressure on the state and to appropriate the resources that the state distributed. If governments lacked efficient instruments with which to select and exclude these demands, they were subjected to an overload of demands and entered a governability crisis (Crozier et al. 1975; Rose 1979). Providing the large interest organizations with privileged access to state resources and involving them in policy-making was therefore a way to hierarchize demands, while at the same time preventing these organizations from exercising their veto power ex post.

Apart from the problems stemming from the operation of the Keynesian welfare state we should remember that in the 1970s the chief priority of economic policy authorities in all Western countries was to combat inflation. The principal anti-inflationary instrument available to those countries which did not pursue monetarist policies was an incomes policy (Flanagan et al. 1983), the effectiveness of which, however, depended on the consensus and participation of the subjects directly concerned. For this reason, therefore, attempts at concertation in the 1970s were mostly centred on incomes policies.

However, it should be pointed out that not all governments of the advanced industrial countries responded to these problems by seeking to create neocorporatist arrangements (Salvati 1982). Some of them tried other approaches, such as seeking to achieve governability through patronage systems which ensured atomistic consensus that was not channelled through the interest organizations. Or they attempted to control distributional conflict by excluding labour from (rather than incorporating it into) the social bloc responsible for managing economic development. Or finally, they sought to reinstate the market and pluralistic pressure politics rather than intensify the public regulation of the economy.

Also, one can argue that the role of the state, and its independent initiative in creating neocorporatist arrangements, has been overestimated. Many neocorporatist analysts have not only attributed an importance to this role, which is excessive when compared with historical fact; they have structured it theoretically as a long-term strategy by the state acting as the 'architect of the political order' (to use Anderson's 1977 expression). From this point of view, it was the state which sought to build a corporatist order – not, of course, by the fiat and repression typical of authoritarian regimes, but with the consent of the organizations involved and by assigning certain privileges to specific interest organizations in exchange for restrictions on their autonomy in the market arena.

However, a key question is left unanswered by this account, or at least it is not answered clearly and satisfactorily: To what extent and under what conditions do interest organizations consider an exchange which creates tensions in their base and restricts their freedom of action as being to their advantage? In fact, those phenomena which the neocorporatist literature calls 'regulation of interest organizations, the delegation to them of public functions, their involvement in political decision-making' are often the outcome of complex exchange relationships among multiple actors, private and public. Each of these actors may take the initiative in structuring the relationship in a stable and co-operative manner, and each of them enters it armed with a strategy which already internalizes systemic constraints and imperatives and leaves it with results proportional to its power.

We must therefore also examine the strategies and calculations of the government's partners – that is, the interest organizations – if we are to understand the development and instability of concertation.[3] I deal first with the problem of how concertation may arise and then examine the conditions which render it more, or less, stable.[4]

It becomes easier to understand why a trade union is, or is not, willing to engage in (or promote) a relationship with the government based on concertation and stable political exchange if we view the decision as the outcome of the rational calculation of costs and benefits.

The advantages deriving to a trade union from a stable political exchange do not consist solely in the increased power of its leaders (on this see Pizzorno 1978; Keeler 1981) or in organizational gains, although such considerations may well be important. The union's principal benefit is its enhanced ability to alter market outcomes so that they work to labour's advantage.

Market outcomes, of course, can also be manipulated by the more traditional method of collective bargaining, the results of which are affected by the organizational resources of the workers. However, although political exchange means that the trade union must to some extent underexploit its power in industrial relations, it may nevertheless prove to be a more attractive option – under certain conditions.

First, state institutions may be more responsive to unions than to employers, and they may also prove more accessible. In other words, trade unions may be able to exercise more power in the political arena than they can in the industrial relations system. This may be due to several factors – for instance, a pro-labour party in office which provides them with political support (as in the European social democracies). Trade unions may therefore find it advantageous to shift the locus of distributional conflict away from industrial relations and into the political system (Korpi and Shalev 1980).

Second, compared with private employers, the state may represent a potentially greater source of benefits for workers (at least relative to the amount of effort required to obtain these benefits). For example, a redistribution of incomes achieved through social reforms and fiscal measures may bring greater advantages for unions than those deriving to them from wage increases in a period of high inflation and liquidity problems for firms. Or, again, employment support by means of industrial and labour policies may prove more effective than attempts to increase staffing levels by bargaining over industrial investment and working hours. In such circumstances, therefore, the unions may regard the opportunities afforded them to influence political decision-making as more crucial than collective bargaining, whatever their relative power in the industrial and political arenas may be.

Third, if the national economy is in recession or is highly exposed to international competition, it may be extremely risky for a trade union (even a strong one) to exploit its bargaining power to the full. Indeed, somewhat paradoxically, the stronger the union, the more likely it is to find itself confronted by an acute dilemma. If the union makes uninhibited use of its organizational strength in pursuit of its members' short-term interests, its disruption of the economy may imperil the very basis of its power, as well as its future ability to obtain benefits for its members. If, however, the union underutilizes its power by moderating its industrial action, it risks provoking widespread internal dissent and weakening the loyalty of its base. Political exchange may consequently be seen as a way out of this dilemma, in that self-restraint in the industrial arena is (or should be) compensated for by the resources furnished by the state.

In short, the chief benefit that a trade union can gain from political exchange with the government is its greater ability to alter the outcomes of the operation of the market, under conditions where resorting to the traditional option of collective bargaining would be less productive or more risky.

If these are the potential benefits of political exchange, what are its potential costs for the trade union? Obviously, political exchange to a certain extent restricts the union's freedom of action in the market arena. Acceptance of this restriction may strain the union's relations with its rank and file and jeopardize its ability to act 'on behalf of' other social groups. In these circumstances the union may incur a variety of costs: the loyalty of its members may weaken, its membership may decline and it may lose its monopoly over the representation tacitly granted to it by social groups other than its own base. These are all serious risks for a trade union – so serious, in fact, that they may render it unwilling to enter a political exchange relationship, for fear of triggering a major crisis of representation.

However, as we shall see, these risks may be less serious the more a union is equipped with the instruments needed to control a crisis. These instruments can take various forms, but they all lower the potential costs of political exchange for the union, thus altering the outcome of its – conscious or otherwise – rational calculation. For example, the monopoly of representation and a high degree of centralization (which are usually considered to be the organizational preconditions for stable concertation) may, from this perspective, be viewed as elements in the union's cost–benefit calculation. By enabling the decision-making process to take place in relative isolation internally to the organization, they may avert open conflict with the rank and file over the appropriate policy to pursue, or they may prevent potential dissent from finding effective organizational forms.

So far, we have assumed that the willingness of actors to enter into that systematic and long-term political exchange which makes concertation possible is based on some form (however crude and covert) of cost–benefit analysis. Yet each of the actors involved may find that its calculation has been faulty. In addition, the ratio between costs and benefits may, for various reasons, rapidly change to its disadvantage. Should this happen, the actor will be tempted to withdraw from the political exchange, or else it will seek to alter the original terms of the deal. In either case, the political exchange becomes unstable and attempts at concertation are thwarted.

The stability of concertation therefore depends on the interaction among the calculations and strategies of the various actors involved – not on the presence or otherwise of the organizational and institutional conditions that the neocorporatist literature holds to be its prerequisites. Put more precisely, the stability of concertation depends on the extent to which both the interest of the actors in a long-term systematic political exchange and their ability to pursue this logic of action are not susceptible to rapid and major changes.

What, then, determines the ability of actors to pursue, continuously and coherently, this logic of action? A strategy of systematic long-term exchange always entails that the actors are able to set limits on the immediate satisfaction of the multiple demands that they represent – by moderating them, selecting among them and aggregating them. Moreover, if these actors are to be reliable parties to long-lasting accords, they must be able to implement this strategy in practice; that is, they must be able to ensure that it achieves the outcome intended and that it is not obstructed by hostile interest groups.

With regard to the trade unions, a first crucial variable is the extent to which they are able to deploy what I earlier called 'the instruments needed to control a crisis of representation'. Framing the problem in these terms highlights the role of the two organizational prerequisites for stable concertation which I mentioned and which figure so prominently in the neocorporatist literature: union centralization and the monopoly of representation. A highly centralized decision-making process necessarily entails a considerable degree of aggregation and adjustment of the demands advanced by the base, so that the rank and file find it difficult to assess the union's responsiveness to their demands. On the other hand, the union's monopoly of representation means that it is practically impossible for dissent to find organizational channels through which to express itself.

However, centralization and the absence of competition are only two of the instruments with which the union can defuse a crisis of representation. Although they are probably the most reliable, their effectiveness has proved variable. And in any case these instruments can be supplemented by others, or even replaced by functional equivalents – that is, by strategies which achieve the same outcome of enabling a trade union to control a crisis of representation (Lehmbruch 1982).

An example of an often effective functional equivalent is the use made by many European trade unions of the ideology of class solidarity as an identity incentive designed to strengthen rank-and-file support for their policies (Regini 1981). Another example is the central co-ordination of plant-level platforms and the constant presence of national union leaders at all levels of decentralized bargaining. This effectively restricts the autonomy of the workers' representatives and therefore the articulation of rank-and-file demands in conflict with national policy. Finally, the absence or precariousness of the formal procedures of trade union democracy, or of the mechanisms which offer the option of 'exit' or 'voice' to dissenters (Hirschman 1970; Lange 1984a), often prevents the majority of workers from expressing their opposition, thereby ensuring that a potential crisis of representation does not degenerate into an open threat to the organization.

A second crucial variable governing a trade union's ability to participate stably in concertation is the extent to which it occupies an oligopolistic position in political bargaining with the government. Whereas the previous variable determined the intensity of representation, this one concerns its extension – that is, the number of functional interests whose only access to political bargaining with the government is mediated by the trade union.

As I have already pointed out (and should become clearer in the first section of Chapter 3), the 'concertation game' differs from pluralistic pressure politics in that it involves only a small number of players. This is why a marked horizontal concentration of interest organizations – as manifest, for example, in the existence of few large-scale industry federations (Lehmbruch 1982) – and the attribution to them of public status (Offe 1981) are often regarded as the necessary conditions for the stability of concertation. Thus, stable concertation requires that only a few large interest groups be given symbolic recognition, ratified as legitimate and incorporated into the institutions responsible for economic policy. Other interests, whether organized or not, are excluded from the political bargaining process. Analyses of Austrian concertation, for example, stress precisely these features as accounting for its exceptional stability (Lehmbruch 1977; Marin 1983).

So far I have discussed the extent to which trade unions are capable of implementing a logic of action based on long-term political exchange. This, we have seen, is an essential condition for the stability of concertation. But, we may ask, to what extent do trade unions see their long-term participation in this kind of exchange as advantageous? Under what conditions will their interest in pursuing this logic of action be sufficiently strong to guarantee their continued participation in concertation, and therefore its stability? From this point of view, the crucial issue is whether the government is willing and able to ensure that the exchange effectively produces the results expected by the unions – that is, policies coherent with their objectives as redefined during the bargaining process.

It is for this reason that the presence of a pro-labour party in office is often regarded as a precondition for stable concertation. However, as with the prerequisites discussed earlier, this tends to short-circuit, so to speak, the argument. In fact, the most important factor governing trade union interest in a stable political exchange is the probability of achieving favourable results. It is certainly true that one such favourable result is that the unions' acceptance of the exchange will prolong a friendly government's term of office. And it is probably true that it is a pro-labour government that the unions normally see as providing the political guarantee that, if they forgo short-term gains, they will in exchange receive other advantages in the future – advantages which, although promised, are necessarily long term and uncertain. The unions detect, that is, a way to overcome the lack of trust which obstructs the will to cooperate (Crouch 1978). Nevertheless, whatever their reasons for preferring a pro-labour government as a partner in political exchange, and whatever the extent of this preference, this condition may rapidly become insufficient.

Even a pro-labour government, in fact, may prove unable to guarantee the output and the outcome of concertation – unable, that is, to implement the decisions taken jointly with the unions and to ensure that they produce the results intended.

First, the government may encounter strong opposition from the social groups penalized by the policies emanating from concertation. Or the government may encounter the more subtle resistance of a public administration hostile to such policies and to the innovations required to implement them. This was the main reason for the failure of concertation during the 'national solidarity' period in Italy (Regini 1984). Second, even a pro-labour government may have to cope with an economic situation so severe that it is forced to change the political agenda previously agreed with the unions or to cut the resources allocated through political bargaining. This, for example, was what happened to the British 'social contract'. After an initial stage of pro-labour measures, the unions found that their benefits had been so drastically curtailed that they were eventually induced to withdraw from the political exchange.

THE CONTENTS AND OUTCOMES OF THE EXCHANGE

The differing degrees of stability in concertation therefore depend, in general, on the changing convenience to the actors – government and organized interests – of giving continuity and systematicity to the political exchange. But it is not just the degree of stability that has proved to be highly variable. The contents and outcomes of political exchange have also shown themselves to be so diversified in the various historical settings in which it has developed as to raise doubts about the legitimacy of such abstract conceptualizations as political exchange and concertation, unless they are accompanied by more concrete specification.

Although the literature has largely ignored this problem, there seems to be no doubt that in the European countries which had some experience of concertation during the 1960s and 1970s, institutional arrangements arose which corresponded to very different power relationships. It is these differences that explain the differences in the formation process, contents and outcomes of political exchange. For our purposes here, a rough outline of three salient historical patterns will suffice.

In the first of these patterns, which I shall call 'stable neocorporatism with the relative hegemony of the labour movement', very strong and initially militant trade unions imposed neo-corporatist political exchange as part of their strategy and managed at least partly to shape its contents. The political regime that corresponded to this system of relationships between trade unions and state was that of the more advanced social democracies: Sweden and Norway and, to a certain extent, Austria.

Until the 1980s, Sweden was a classic example of the pattern of stable neocorporatism based on an exchange largely directed and controlled by the labour movement. Many studies have been made of the Swedish case (see, e.g., Korpi 1978; Martin 1979; Stephens 1979), and the reader is referred to them for a detailed description (on Austria, see Marin 1983). I shall restrict myself here to a brief examination of some very general features of this model.

When a deal which we would today call neocorporatist was first struck in the 1930s, the Swedish working class was very strong and militant. According to the calculations of Korpi and Shalev (1980), although statistics show that in the period from 1946 to 1976 Sweden registered the fewest strikes among eighteen industrial countries, the country had the greatest number of strikes in 1900–13, and still occupied ninth place in 1919–38. The opportunities to shape economic and social policies provided by the social democratic party's ascent to government, however, persuaded the Swedish labour movement to prioritize the political system as the arena in which to pursue its goals of full employment and equality. Given the party's extremely long term of office, these goals were for the most part achieved. Like other European countries, postwar Sweden not only enjoyed full employment but witnessed the major development of its welfare state. More important, however, the action of its government had large-scale redistributive effects (Korpi and Shalev 1980). Consequently, the political exchange practised by the Swedish trade unions – or, if one prefers, their class compromise – by no means weakened them. In the postwar period, in terms of both union membership and the percentage of votes for the parties of the Left, the Swedish labour movement remained the strongest of all those in the Western countries. Against this background, the sharp decline of industrial conflict should be interpreted not as a symptom of trade-union weakness, but as an effect of the shifting of conflict from the industrial arena to the political system.

Not only were the Swedish unions not weakened by their acceptance of a long-term deal, but, in contrast to the other types of neocorporatist arrangement that I discuss later, they were largely able to determine the contents of the exchange. In collective bargaining, they were to a great extent able to impose their egalitarian goals by pursuing a solidaristic wage policy. In their relations with government, they managed to shift the focus from simple co-operation to an incomes policy, to the development of an active labour policy and social security which matched their strategic objectives and which they largely shaped. As with all experiences of concertation, the Swedish model revealed its limitations and began to disintegrate in the 1980s and 1990s for reasons common to the other industrial democracies (see Chapter 5). Yet it is still to this model that one must refer as an ideal-typical case of stable neocorporatism under labour hegemony.

The second historical pattern, one might call 'the stable incorporation of the working class into economic policy formation in a subordinate position'. Examples of this pattern are provided by Switzerland and Holland (Scholten 1987; Blaas 1992). The labour movements in these countries were much weaker in both the industrial arena and the political system. Nevertheless, after the Second World War, the parties of the Left in these countries were not entirely excluded from government coalitions, as happened in France and in Italy from 1948 until the early 1960s. Opportunities for labour movements to obtain substantial advantages through the state were far fewer than in Sweden – both because of the limited and sporadic influence of the movements on the governments and because they were too weak to impose their goals on economic and social policy. However, it was precisely this weakness, combined with government policies offering involvement and co-operation rather than political isolation, that dissuaded the unions from rejecting these offers and from adopting an alternative, more adversarial strategy. The class compromise therefore came about in a situation of power relationships which were generally weighted against the labour movement – not, as in the previous case, under its relative hegemony.

The low level of industrial conflict in these countries was a further aspect of the weakness and subordination of the unions; it did not, as in Sweden, result from a strategic choice. Not coincidentally, these are the countries most frequently cited by those theoreticians of neocorporatism who see its essence as the incorporation of the unions into tripartite bodies, as their subordinate involvement in public institutions and as restrictions on their freedom of action exchanged for the state's delegation to them of public functions. Not only were the trade unions forced to exercise self-restraint in advancing their claims and to comply with the 'general interest', and also obliged to collaborate because viable alternatives were lacking; their co-operation also resulted in the strong institutionalization of their relationships with the state. The core of the neocorporatist accord was the incomes policy (Panitch 1977) – which in practice meant a relatively moderate wage policy without any major trade-offs in terms of active labour policies and social policy. The redistributive effects of state intervention were overall less significant in these countries than in those of the first group (Korpi and Shalev 1980).

Because of these features, the neocorporatist accord was decidedly less attractive to the unions than it was in Sweden. Nevertheless, in this case too it displayed a certain stability – for various reasons which are widely discussed in the literature (Katzenstein 1984; Parri 1987; Scholten 1987). Suffice it to point out that the economic expansion of the postwar years enabled all the interests penalized by this accord to recoup their losses, while the centralization and bureaucratization of the unions insulated them against pressures from the rank and file, and the large number of immigrants in these countries and their ethnic-linguistic divisions sectorialized and isolated protest.

We may call the third historical pattern 'unstable neocorporatism as a consequence of stalemated political exchange'. This was the pattern followed by countries like Great Britain, Denmark and Italy in the late 1970s and early 1980s, countries which, in postwar years, have had rather strong and militant labour movements. The levels of unionization in these countries and the electoral strength of the political Left mean that they more closely resembled the first of the two patterns than the second (see again Korpi and Shalev 1980).

However, there have been many fewer opportunities for the unions to obtain benefits by political means such that they are persuaded that institutionalized co-operation is in their interest. In Great Britain, an alternating sequence of Labour and Conservative governments meant that opportunities for the unions to influence economic and social policies became sporadic. In Denmark, the mixed electoral fortunes of the Social Democratic Party, which lost votes both to the Left and to the Progress Party, had the same effect. Finally, Italian governments in the 1970s and 1980s, while in constant need of legitimation by the unions and therefore never overtly antilabour, were not in a position to strike a long-term deal with the unions or even to make consistently pro-labour choices (Regini 1984, 1987). In all three cases, the trade unions did not judge pro-labour governments to be stable and powerful enough to guarantee favourable outcomes of long-term social pacts.

In the British case, moreover, the decentralized structure of industrial relations meant that it was difficult to force trade-union action to comply with centralized agreements. One may therefore say that although attempts to find a stable neocorporatist accord were constantly on the agenda, they were invariably unsuccessful (Crouch 1977).

Unlike the first two groups, these countries experienced rather high levels of industrial conflict and for long periods. This demonstrates, on the one hand, the difficulties the unions faced in obtaining by political means advantages sufficient to induce them to moderate their claims, even more so to develop a culture of co-operation; it shows, on the other, their enduring ability to mobilize workers. The redistributive effects of government policies were, moreover, much less marked than in the other countries. The unions therefore had less reason to believe that their institutionalized participation would be effectively compensated by greater social equality. This explains why political exchange was stalemated and why, therefore, neocorporatist arrangements were intrinsically unstable.

3

Organized interests and public policies

Concertation, with its various patterns discussed in the preceding chapter, represents one possible type of relationship between state and organized interests in the advanced industrial democracies. In this chapter I shall analyse the ways in which these organizations can participate first in policy-making and then in policy implementation. The strategies of political exchange and concertation – which were pivotal to the model of the centralized political regulation of the economy and hence attracted most attention from students of the relationship between economy and society in the 1970s and 1980s – will thus be framed in a broader typology which highlights their features and specific effects.

ORGANIZED INTERESTS AND POLICY-MAKING

Organized social interests are able to condition regulatory intervention by the state in various ways and to various extents. Of course, the observation that social classes and groups influence state action according to the resources available to them is by no means a new or controversial one. But what I shall seek to show in this section is that there exists another, perhaps less obvious relationship. Put briefly, depending on the type of interaction that takes place between organized interests and state institutions in the public policy-making process, the abilities of these interests to influence its outcomes will vary. In other words, although the differences in the power wielded by social groups in society account, to a large extent, for their various abilities to condition public policy, these abilities are in turn mediated by the forms assumed by their relationship with the institutions that exercise decision-making power. In what follows, therefore, I shall propose a typology of policy-making based on a range of possible relationships between social interests and public decision centres.[1]

The literature presents various images of policy-making, which correspond in part to different analytical perspectives (the public-policy approach or the neocorporatist one) or disciplinary traditions. To impose some order on this rather confused situation, I shall base my analysis on two of the principal analytical dimensions underlying the relationships between social interests and state institutions in the process of public policy-making. Each of these dimensions can be conceived as a continuum.

The first of them is the extent to which the decisional process is insulated against or secluded from pressure by social interests. In a highly insulated policy-making process, inputs in the form of social demands are filtered, and sometimes profoundly altered, by the objectives and culture of the decision-makers. As a result, the outputs no longer simply reflect the demands advanced by the various social interest groups (or their power relationships); instead, they reflect the way that their representatives have redefined them and subordinated them to what they construe as being in the institutional interest – or at least in the common interest of the decision-makers. A high degree of insulation does not necessarily mean that the representatives of social interests are excluded from the decision process (indeed, they are often stable and institutionally sanctioned participants in it), but rather that their actions tend to comply with the logic I have just described. Highly insulated decision situations are particularly conducive to the development of co-operative games among the participants. However, these two features – high insulation and co-operation – do not always coincide. As we shall see, even in situations of low insulation, actors may engage in forms of distributive collusion based on 'satisficing' rather than 'maximizing' logic (Simon 1947).

At the two extremes of the insulation/noninsulation continuum, there is practically no interaction between interests and institutions. When insulation is at its maximum, the institutions pursue wholly public objectives, and representatives of private interests are largely excluded from the determination of such objectives. More typical of authoritarian regimes, this situation rarely arises in democratic political systems, although what Salvati (1982) has called 'government by decree' in describing the French case resembles it rather closely. At the other end of the continuum, the decision process is minimally insulated against social interests when some of the latter are allowed to produce public policies directly. This is the case – widely studied in neocorporatist literature – of the 'delegation of public functions to private governments' (Streeck and Schmitter 1985).[2]

However, as I have said, interaction between interests and institutions in the decision process is practically nonexistent in the two extreme cases. They are therefore of little relevance to my present discussion. The types of policy-making that I instead intend to discuss relate to intermediate (although differentiated) situations along the continuum of low to high insulation; these I shall call, for reasons given later, 'pluralistic pressure' and 'policy network'.

The second dimension is the degree of comprehensiveness (or, vice versa, of segmentation) of the decision process. Very comprehensive policy-making is typified by a large aggregation of interests which constitute the input to the decision process and, especially, by a close interdependence among its outputs, in the sense that the policies produced are globalistic and intersectoral (Regonini 1985), or at least closely intermeshed.

The logical extremes of this continuum are inevitably abstract and are of little relevance to empirical inquiry. Maximum comprehensiveness in policy-making is achieved in cases of the global planning of the economy. This, however, is largely alien to the experience of the industrial democracies. At the other extreme, maximum segmentation occurs when public policies are altogether devoid of coherence: when they fail to follow any overall logic but simply respond to a micro-corporatist fragmentation of public or private interests.

Located along this dimension, too, are intermediate cases which are much more important from an empirical point of view. I discuss them in detail later. A situation of low comprehensiveness generally occurs in distributive policy-making (Dente and Regonini 1989), which has been described as typical of 'spoils system governance' (Amato 1976). A highly comprehensive situation, by contrast, is one in which forms of oligopolistic bargaining predominate.

Within the space marked out by these two dimensions, three types of policy-making emerge as particularly important in terms of the relationships between social interests and the decision centres responsible for public policy-making (see Figure 1).

a. The model of pluralistic pressure/spoils system governance is well known to political scientists: it is one in which social interests are represented by a multiplicity of associations. Although the aggregative capacity of these associations is variable, the overall aggregation of inputs to the decision process is very low. The outputs are segmented because, given the highly fragmented nature of the representation of interests, each association seeks to satisfy limited demands while neglecting to establish linkages with other policy areas.

On the other hand, the decision centres (be these the parliament and parliamentary commissions, the government or the public administration) are highly susceptible to private pressures. In theory, each interest group manages to shape public policies proportionately to its strength – that is, in proportion to the resources that it is able to deploy in the political market. In some countries, the political parties perform a vital role in mediating between fragmented social demands and the decision-making institutions (Pasquino 1986, 1989). When pluralistic pressure/spoils system governance predominates,

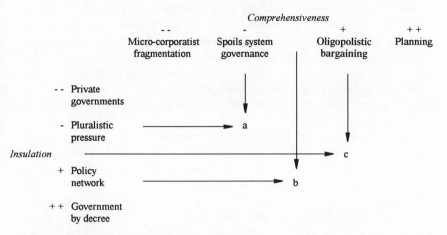

Figure 1. Types of interaction between organized interests and decision centres in the production of public policies.

however, the political parties do not substantially influence the natural outcomes of the power relationships among interests. 'The interests express appropriative demands and their political representatives restrict themselves to issuing, through the institutional decision centres, responses exactly symmetrical to those demands, each of them pushing for the interests from which it believes its support comes' (Amato 1976: 170–1). The parties weigh the resources of the contenders and accordingly articulate their demands to the political system in realistic terms.

Of the three models of public policy-making under discussion here, therefore, this is the one in which the structure of the decision process (i.e., the type of relationship between organized interests and institutions) modifies the direct translation of social demands into policies the least. Demands are subject to alterations which reflect power relationships, but not ones attributable to the manner in which these demands are processed. This model is usually characterized by sporadic competition among interest groups in which manifold pressures contend to divide up the state's resources and to condition its authority. However, when costs can be externalized or spread, distributive collusion may arise in which each actor manages to satisfy its demands and collaborates for this purpose with the others.

b. The model of the policy community or policy network is an image of the decision process developed by public-policy studies.[3] Here, too, the production of public policies tends to be rather segmented. The term 'policy network' itself implies that the decision process is confined to the contents of a specific policy area and cannot extend beyond them. Nevertheless, the policy area may also be defined in broad terms (e.g., labour problems or educational issues), and in this case account must presumably be taken of relationships with other networks. This intermediate level of comprehensiveness of output is probably matched by a markedly variable degree of aggregation among the interests acting as inputs to the decision process. It is therefore not its position on the comprehensiveness/segmentation continuum that defines this type of public policy-making.

This model's essential difference with respect to pluralistic pressure/spoils system governance is that in this case the decision process is solidly insulated against external demands. This is not to imply that organized interests are excluded from policy-making or that they are unable to influence it. But when the representatives of these interests join the network of relationships centred on a particular policy area, they change their logic of action. And so do the other actors in the network (representatives of other interests and of the political parties, bureaucrats). As experts in a particular area, these possess scarce resources; they are all concerned to ensure that the policy of interest to them stands high on the political agenda; and they engage in co-operative game-playing, which may induce them to redefine their original goals in order to create one common to all the members of the network. Involvement in the construction of the single institutional goal comes to predominate over the task of representing demands.

In this type of policy-making, therefore, the structure of the decision process significantly alters the probability of social demands being translated directly into policies. Rather than sporadic competition and pressures, a logic of stable co-operation among interest representatives, and between these and the institutions, predominates in public-policy production. Moreover, should some other logic manage to impose itself, the model breaks down and other forms of policy-making take over (Regonini 1985).

c. We come finally to the model of oligopolistic bargaining. This derives in part from the neocorporatist literature – and is in fact the one that best captures the patterns of political exchange discussed in the preceding chapter – although it is not narrowly tied to it.

What distinguishes this model from the two preceding ones is, first, that not all interests enter the political arena in fragmentary form. There are certain large encompassing organizations which are able to pre-mediate among multiple social interests and thus transmit them in aggregate form to policy-making institutions. Much the same may occur as a result of the action of mass political parties, which are still able to aggregate social demand as they have always done in the past (Kircheimer 1966), rather than simply turn into 'catch-all' parties. When these actors participate in the decision process, they may follow a logic which takes account of the interdependencies between decisions in one area of policy-making and those to be taken in another. Unlike fragmented interest groups and sectoral experts, they may find it convenient to give priority to the congruence among decisions taken in different policy areas. This is possible if only actors with these characteristics participate in the production of public policies, if they are few in number and if they agree to exclude all others. For this reason one may talk about oligopolistic bargaining among certain actors granted privileged access to the state's resources.[4]

Second, these actors follow a logic of interest representation, not one of seeking to construct an institutional goal. They must therefore transmit, at least in part, the demands of their members or constituency. However, and this the neocorporatist literature has shown very clearly, alongside their representative function, the large encompassing organizations also perform the role of controlling their members' demands. This they do for two main reasons: first, because the high degree of aggregation of interests requires that intra-organizational decision processes be protected against 'excessive' influence by the represented; and second, because if these organizations are to preserve their status as oligopolist participants (i.e., if they are to preserve their privileged access to state resources), they must be able to guarantee that those they represent will comply with the decisions taken at the peak. Therefore, in this type of public policy-making, the level of insulation against social demands is intermediate with respect to those of the other two types. The need for representation and the need for control counterbalance each other. If they do not do so, contradictions arise which may destabilize this form of policy-making.

In public policy-making based on oligopolistic bargaining, then, the decision process to some extent alters social demands. The relationships among the interest-representing actors, and between these and the institutions, are typified by a mixture of competition (or conflict) and co-operation; that is to say, these relationships have a style which the notion of concertation captures rather well.

Obviously, actors apart from the representatives of social interests and the institutions may be involved in the production of public policies. In particular, political parties and technical bureaucracies may also participate, with their own interests and with their own resources. Theoretically, each of these actors may come to dominate the decision process – if by dominance we mean the ability to set the agenda and to deploy the resources necessary to secure the outcome desired. The aim of this typology, however, is not to predict the influence of various actors on policy-making, although the particular way in which the relationship between interests and institutions is structured may largely preclude dominance by certain of them.[5] This observation, in fact, reveals that it is also highly unlikely that one particular actor will be able to dominate the entire production of public policies, unless one or more of the types of policy-making discussed here are extraneous to a specific political system.[6]

The principal aim of my discussion so far has been to complete the analysis set out in Chapters 1 and 2. We may now examine its capacity to interpret specific national cases. By way of example, I shall try to establish the extent to which the three models outlined in the preceding paragraphs are able to capture the policy-making process in Italy.

For years, the Italian political system has been described as fiercely conflictual and ideologically polarized (Sartori 1966), but it has also been characterized by distributive practices which cement the ruling social bloc together and compensate those excluded from the decision process (Amato 1976). The type of public-policy production apparently best suited to a political system of this kind is pluralistic pressure/spoils system governance (and in fact numerous authors cite this as the predominant model in Italy, although they use different terminologies). In Italy, moreover, interests display a relatively high degree of fragmentation, and the country's public institutions are extremely permeable. Nor does the significant role traditionally performed by the political parties contrast with this model, since they have been able to act as the principal agent of social mediation while simultaneously exerting a decisive influence over the functioning of the institutions. Although mediated by the political parties, therefore, it is highly probable that social demands will translate directly into public policies mirroring power relationships in society, without being significantly filtered by the decision process.

More in-depth studies, however, have shown that although this model is appropriate for some areas – for instance, industrial policies (Ferrera 1989; Maraffi 1987 for the local level) – it is not so for others. First of all, since the mid-1970s various attempts have been made to flank the pluralistic pressure/spoils system model with oligopolistic bargaining in several policy areas (incomes policies, industrial and labour policies, pensions). These attempts have been widely reported in the literature and given various interpretations (see, e.g., Regini 1987; Cella 1989). In brief, however, one may say that the oligopolistic bargaining model has never fully managed to establish itself. Organized interests have never been sufficiently strong to impose it, either on other actors or on those they represent; and the state has found it difficult to provide the guarantees and compensation necessary for the model to work. Oligopolistic bargaining, however, is still on the political agenda in Italy – as the long-drawn-out tripartite negotiation on incomes policy in 1992–3 has shown – and will probably be proposed again for other policies in the future, with variable outcomes.

Second, many policy areas have apparently been dominated by a type of public-policy production that closely resembles the policy network model (Regonini 1985; Addis 1987; see also Regalia 1987 and Regonini 1987 for the local level). As I have said, this is not to imply that, here too, the parties are not central to the decision process. But the logic adopted by their representatives has tended more towards relatively stable co-operation with the other public and private actors concerned with a particular policy than towards competition based on partisan allegiance and designed to strengthen their own organizations.

This appears to contradict the image of conflict and polarization that has, until recently, attached to Italian politics. However, it is possible to conceive of the two phenomena as closely intertwined. A highly conflictual and polarized political system would risk paralysis, in fact, if the production of public policies followed the logic of partisan politics – the logic, that is, of competition for the votes of the electorate. Instead, as we have seen, even party representatives in individual policy areas often follow different kinds of logic, and these are based on segmentation and insulation and characterized by co-operative game-playing. This may perhaps be the result of 'goal displacement' (Selznick 1957), that is, a situation where the party organization shifts its original goals. Or it may be due to the fact that, in many policy areas, politicians have no distinct order of preferences and therefore find it more rational to give priority to membership of the policy network – where they are experts and can influence the position of the party to which they belong – rather than to the goals of their organizations, since here the outcomes of their action are difficult to assess (Dente and Regonini 1989). However, it is more likely due to the strategy of the parties and large interest organizations which, although their political rhetoric stresses competition or conflict, in the practical realities of policy-making consent to and encourage co-operative game-playing in order to avert decisional stalemate – as long as this does not create costs higher than those of the stalemate itself.

ORGANIZED INTERESTS AND POLICY IMPLEMENTATION

Having analysed the policy-making phase, I now turn to the relationships that may arise between organized interests and public institutions in the implementation of public policies.[7] What forms can the interaction between organized interests and public institutions take? In other words, what relationships emerge in the implementation of policies envisaging a potential or actual role for these interests – sometimes a role stipulated by law? What effects does the adoption of a specific form of interaction have on the implementation of policies and on the operational styles of administrative bodies? And what are its feedback effects on the more general goals pursued by the interest organizations and on their organizational dynamics?

One may begin by asking whether the various images of the relationship between institutions and organized interests in the production of public policies that I examined in the preceding section also grasp the variability in the relationships between these same actors in the implementation of such policies. The findings of some of the relatively few studies on organized interests and policy implementation (regarding Italy, see Maraffi 1987; Regalia 1987; Regonini 1987) prompt one to answer that they cannot. To understand why, we should remember that the three models discussed in the preceding section hinge on two analytical dimensions which are indeed significant in the policy-making stage but probably not in the policy implementation one. The first dimension was, it will be recalled, the degree to which the decision process is insulated against or separate from pressure by social interests. The second dimension was the comprehensiveness (or, vice versa, the segmentation) of the decision process. The empirical results of the above-mentioned studies of the relationships between trade unions and public institutions reveal extremely low levels of comprehensiveness and insulation.

These findings raise a number of interesting issues, which unfortunately I can deal with only briefly here. First, it comes as no surprise that policy implementation should, by its very nature, be segmented and with limited comprehensiveness in the above sense. Whereas globalistic and intersectoral policies (e.g., those comprising package deals) can indeed be produced during the formation stage, it is highly likely that their implementation will require specific measures. Of course, this is not to say that the implementation of certain provisions may not be closely connected – in both the temporal and qualitative sense – with the implementation of others, especially when the implementers operate within wide margins of discretion. But this is difficult to achieve and rarely happens.

Second, whatever room may exist for the alteration or reinterpretation of demands in the formation phase of public policies, insulating them against social pressures is apparently far more difficult in the implementation stage. Indeed, the need to maximize the interests of all the social partners represented is, in the opinion of many observers, the principal reason for the frequent inefficiency of public-service delivery and its high cost. This suggests that the redefinition of private interests in order to render them compatible with shared goals and with institutional interests – something which frequently happens in the formation stage of public policies – has principally the symbolic value of 'demonstrating willingness'; and it is difficult for this to predominate in the implementation stage.

Thus, the analytical framework developed to interpret policy-making is unable to capture variations in the relationships between organized interests and public institutions in the implementation stage as well. Instead, the analytical dimensions most relevant to analysis of these relationships seem to be the following.

The first relates to the type of game-playing that takes place among the participants in policy implementation – that is, among the representatives of social interests with access to it, and between these and the representatives of the competent political and administrative institutions. It is possible to identify two principal kinds of games among these actors, which I shall call 'co-operation games' and 'distinction games'.

Co-operation games comprise those situations in which public policies are implemented by means of unanimous and distributive decisions signalling collusion among the participants. However, they also include cases in which co-operation signals an attempt by the participants to streamline policy implementation by adopting shared rules of the game – or at any rate an attempt to pursue goals which transcend the simple maximization of interests. This category also includes situations in which the purpose of co-operation is the exchange of legitimation and political support among participants.

Distinction games are those situations in which the actors' strategies are, and remain, profoundly different. This may generate competition, or even open conflict, over the ways in which the implementation should come about. Alternatively, one or more of the potential actors may be effectively extraneous to the process – either because it has been excluded from the privileged relationships established among the other actors or because it has deliberately chosen to abstain. Or again, there may be a more or less ritual stand-off among the participants which is intended more to reaffirm principles than to obtain results.

The second dimension concerns the main content of the relationships among the participants in policy implementation. The interaction between social interests and public institutions may, in fact, have two different functions. The first is to perform specific tasks confined to the implementation of public policies. The second is politico-symbolic in nature and serves to exchange legitimation or, instead, to provide a public arena in which contrasting strategies are assessed.

These two functions, moreover, correspond to ambivalent goals pursued by the actors. Organized interests seek to establish a relationship with public institutions, either to influence policy implementation and therefore the distribution of state resources in their favour and of the groups they represent, or to achieve greater recognition and thereby increase their power. The administrative institutions which involve organized interests in policy implementation, for their part, set themselves different goals at the same time: on the one hand, they seek to ensure the prior acceptance of policies by those target social groups which could otherwise cause their failure, as well as to exploit their information resources; on the other, they seek to increase their levels of social legitimation and of consensus for their actions. Depending on which of these two aspects predominates in the actors' goals, the effective content of the relationships between organized interests and public institutions will change.

If we now cross-reference the two analytical dimensions just described, we obtain the scheme shown in Figure 2, which sets out the four different kinds of interaction between social interests and public institutions. These I shall call 'identity differentiation', 'demonstrative consensus', 'opposition in implementation' and 'implementative collaboration'.

This typology can be used to address the crucial question of the outcomes of the interaction between organized interests and public institutions – bearing in mind, of course, that the variety of forms assumed by the interaction also corresponds to the plurality of these actors' goals and strategies. How successful is policy implementation when organized interests are involved in the process? Put more specifically (drawing on the terminology of public-policy studies): what changes in the output, outcome and impact of public policies can be considered to be specific consequences of the participation of these interests in their implementation?

It seems quite obvious that when the relationships between social interests and public institutions assume predominantly politico-symbolic contents, the concrete results of policy implementation will be meagre. Or else the former will be unable to condition effectively the ways in which policies are put into practice. More interesting are the two types of relationship which I have called implementative collaboration and opposition in implementation. When the actors confine their interaction to the implementation of specific contents of a particular policy, what consequences does the adoption of co-operation strategies, or alternatively of distinction strategies, have on the public institutions' style of action? In particular, what are the differing effects of these strategies on the efficiency of the public institutions and the speed with which they perform their tasks?

One of the principal assumptions of the neocorporatist literature is that co-operation institutionalized into public bodies has the effect of transforming representative organizations into champions of the general interest, thus enabling distributive conflict to be internalized. The price, however, is that the decision-making process becomes sluggish. For this reason, it is argued, concertation is always a second-best solution, one which each actor accepts when it is unable to impose its preferred solution but which it is ready to sacrifice in order to accelerate decision-making when power relationships

	Distinction games	Co-operation games
Politico-symbolic contents	Identity differentiation	Demonstrative consensus
Specific contents of implementation	Opposition in implementation	Implementative collaboration

Figure 2. Types of interaction between organized interests and public institutions in policy implementation.

have shifted decisively in its favour. However, the findings of the Italian research studies cited earlier seem to suggest the reverse. I shall now draw on these studies to illustrate briefly the consequences of the interaction between organized interests and public institutions in policy implementation. In particular, what I have called 'implementative collaboration' appears to introduce a certain amount of efficiency and speed into policy implementation, while it does not favour the internalization of shared constraints and interests by the actors concerned.

Consider the example of the provincial committees for administering the Wages Guarantee Fund, studied by Ida Regalia (1987). All three of the provincial cases examined revealed an operational style marked by a fair degree of efficiency: meetings were frequent and regular; there was always a quorum: there was practically no backlog of work; applications were dealt with extremely quickly; all the commissioners took great care to update their files with precedents, rulings and relevant information. That this efficiency was no accident, but rather the direct consequence of the inclusion of the social partners on the committee, was demonstrated by the fact that applications for the wages fund were usually submitted already complete with the documentation necessary for their appraisal. This was because the interest organizations prodded their members into producing this information, and thus notably accelerated the inquiry procedure.

Or consider the case of INPS (the Italian public institute administering pensions) studied by Gloria Regonini (1987). This study, too, concludes that management controlled by the social partners, and with a trade-union majority, certainly did not slow down the institute's decision-making processes. On the one hand, the bureaucracy of the institute preserved de facto monopoly over decisions as to what was legitimate and viable, so that the representatives of the social partners on the executive committee were unable to change its traditional practices. On the other, the fact that the INPS managers belonged to the network of the national trade unions and their associated political parties accelerated the process of legislation-implementation-error correction by new legislative measures.

However, the relative rapidity of the decision-making process by no means led to an enhanced capacity to achieve institutional goals; nor was it the result of the internalization of a public interest by all the actors involved. Rather, it was the outcome of a distributive pact among the interests represented in the implementation process. This, therefore, was efficiency founded on collusion between social interests and representatives of the political and administrative institutions. This emerges clearly with regard to the normal functioning of INPS and its provincial and regional committees. The proof by default comes when, for external reasons, the collusion breaks down and relationships turn into opposition in implementation – as happened over the issues of how to combat the evasion of welfare contributions and whether to allow the deferment of payment. Then the decision-making process becomes more sluggish.

Not dissimilar is the case of the provincial committees responsible for administering the Wages Guarantee Fund. Here, in fact, apparently one goal was shared by all the members of these bodies: verifying the formal correctness of applications to the fund. One might therefore argue that, in this case, a public interest was indeed internalized. However, the fact remains that the results were highly distributive and that they were the more so the more efficiently the committee did its work.

Apart from the effects exerted by the participation of organized interests in policy implementation on the operational styles of the public institutions, we should also briefly examine its feedback effects on the organized interests themselves. One might expect, in fact, their differing degrees of managerial responsibility in policy implementation to affect the behaviour of organized interests, induce them to redefine their goals and influence their organizational dynamics. Yet the empirical evidence already cited does not support this conclusion.

With regard to the types of relationship that I have called identity differentiation and demonstrative consensus, this is not difficult to explain. When the involvement of organized interests in policy implementation is predominantly politico-symbolic in nature, so that it does not entail specific responsibilities and allows the simple reaffirmation of general principles, there is no reason to expect repercussions internal to them. In certain cases, the apparent indifference of interest organizations to consolidating and institutionalizing their relationships with public institutions may conceal a desire to avoid strains on their relationship with the rank and file and on their traditional bargaining procedures.

For example, industrial policies are a minefield for both trade unions and employers' associations. The goals normally attributed to these policies by public institutions – that is, the modernization and rationalization of industry – often conflict with the traditional views of them held both by trade-union organizations (for whom the chief problem is job protection in situations of company crisis) and by employers (who willingly accept the distributive aspects of these policies, but reject the more active role by the state that they frequently incorporate). In this case, one can legitimately argue that less vigorous interaction, based more on routine consultations than on managerial responsibilities, may be in the interests of both the public institutions and the social interests involved. They prefer, therefore, forms of external pressure on the public institutions which yield limited benefits but without constraints and without institutional implications (Maraffi 1987).

It is more difficult to explain why there are also negligible feedback effects in those cases where the involvement of the interest organizations in public-policy implementation is major and highly institutionalized. In particular, the logic of action pursued by their representatives in the public bodies does not seem to have significant effects on the external strategies of the organizations themselves. One possible interpretation is that a kind of tacit agreement has been reached between these representatives and their organizations whereby the noninterference of the latter in the functions of the former will be matched by an undertaking that they will not seek to influence the drawing-up of strategies.

Large interest organizations, moreover, are complex actors, whose criterion for regulating their internal relationships is more often the division of tasks than imperative co-ordination, although there are numerous intermediate forms between these two extremes. Their operations consequently often take place in watertight compartments, so that it is difficult for reciprocal conditioning between them to occur.

4

An anomalous case? State, economy and organized interests in Italy

The dynamics of the relationships between state and economy examined in Chapter 1 concern to some extent all the advanced industrial democracies. Therefore, Italy has also seen the growth and decline of the Keynesian welfare state. However, in both scientific and political debate, one notes a certain reticence, almost discomfiture, in applying this analytical category to Italy – so much so that it is frequently accompanied by stress on the country's 'peculiarity'.

Whereas 'American exceptionalism' and the *Modell Deutschland* – to cite two examples of categories equally widespread in analysis of these two national cases, respectively – assume the status of real conceptual tools, rather than being treated as national variants of a general pattern, the 'Italian case' (Cavazza and Graubard 1974; Lange and Tarrow 1980; Lange and Regini 1989) has come to symbolize the difficulty of applying any analytical category developed for the purposes of comparison. In fact, with respect to the models used in comparative analysis, interpretation of the Italian case and of its evolution consists mainly in highlighting a series of 'shifts' within a context considered, for reasons that are rather unclear, to be more multiform and complex than that of other countries and which therefore cannot be captured by oversimplified concepts.

HAS THERE EVER BEEN A KEYNESIAN WELFARE STATE IN ITALY?

First of all, there is the widely held opinion (Amato 1976; Cassese 1987) that, in Italy, public intervention in the economy is both more extensive than in other Western countries and extremely inefficient, in that it is unable to produce a coherent and comprehensive economic policy.

Not only are the boundaries of the 'state as entrepreneur' (i.e., the public ownership of companies), and therefore also its ability to control the economic development of the country, extremely broad in comparative terms, but the

Italian state also has potentially far-reaching instruments at its disposal for the regulation of the economy. Just as far-reaching is its ability to allocate economic resources directly, because of an abnormally large public debt and a type of public expenditure which gives priority to money transfers over services. Take, for example, labour policies (for an analysis see Reyneri 1989). If one jointly considers the legal and administrative instruments enabling the public control of the labour market, the allocation of state resources to the Wages Guarantee Fund, early retirement funds and so on, and the direct regulation that takes place in the public sector and in that of state-controlled enterprises, one must conclude that the Italian state is, theoretically, among the most interventionist in the Western world.

However, in the formation of these and other public policies, it is the system of pluralistic pressure/spoils system governance (see Chapter 3) that predominates. The effect of this system is to render the Italian economic policy authorities less able than their counterparts in other countries to elaborate and pursue a long-term, coherent and overall design. In fact, it makes these decision centres highly permeable to private interests and often gives rise to outright distributive collusion, which systematically thwarts all attempts to create a design of this kind.

Second, as far as Keynesian policies in Italy are concerned, it is precisely the absence of this comprehensive long-term design that has been responsible for their fragility and uncertainty. Not by chance have these policies been described as a 'weak version of Keynesianism' (Bordogna and Provasi 1984) – a description applicable not only to Italy but also to such other advanced industrial democracies as the United States (see, however, Salvati 1982). The weakness of Keynesian policies in Italy, moreover, has been matched by the majority role of the reformist political forces that have most vigorously promoted them. And, furthermore, those government coalitions which have actually incorporated some significant elements of Keynesianism into their programmes have been short-lived and beset with difficulties. The Keynesian objectives of the Centre–Left governments of the early 1960s, in particular, ended up as the recessionary measures of 1963 (Salvati 1980). The fact that these measures were again introduced in 1973 demonstrates that the objective of full employment has never been taken as truly binding in Italy.

Third, is it possible to talk of the development of a welfare state in Italy? The answer is undoubtedly yes if one looks at the figures on social expenditure relative to GDP, which place Italy in an intermediate position among the advanced industrial countries. But what type of welfare state has this expenditure given rise to? Here again, the scientific debate emphasizes the difficulties and doubts that arise when traditional typologies are applied to Italy. If we use

Titmuss's (1974) categories (those most widely used, albeit with some variants, in the international literature), the Italian system of social policy cannot be easily assimilated to any of his three models: neither to the residual model, nor to the meritocratic-particularist one, nor, especially, to the institutional-redistributive one. In the 1960s and 1970s the Italian system acquired certain universalistic-egalitarian features (e.g., the extension of compulsory schooling and the creation of the national health service in 1978) typical of the institutional-redistributive model. But overall it continued to be particularist-corporatist in character (as was very evident, for example, in the progressive extension of pension schemes to the most diverse social and occupational groups, at different times and with different contribution–benefit ratios), while its universalistic aspects were implemented using clientelistic methods. Therefore, in this case too, it has been necessary to invent new categories, such as the 'particularistic-clientelistic' system, in order to include the Italian case within a broader typology (Ascoli 1984; Ferrera 1984; Paci 1989).

Finally, debate over possible remedies for the crisis of the Keynesian welfare state has taken its own specific form in Italy, especially regarding the strategies suggested by reformist political groups. As we saw at the end of Chapter 1, the principal response to the crisis by most of the European Left was not to cut back welfare benefits; nor was it to improve the efficiency and quality of the services provided by the state. Priority was given, instead, to intervention in the labour market and in the employment relationship – that is, action intended to redistribute opportunities for work among a larger portion of the population, to restore full employment and to improve the quality of the employment relationship.

Although Italian debate on possible solutions to the welfare state crisis also considered these objectives, it nevertheless gave priority to other goals. The reason is that the Italian welfare system did not spring from the egalitarian-solidaristic-universalistic vision of a strong labour movement as it did in the countries of social democratic tradition. In fact, it displays none of these traits. Social policy measures in Italy have adhered to the logic of providing support for various social groups in order to secure their political consensus. The Italian recipe has been the extreme fragmentation of benefits and heavy welfare dependency by beneficiaries, on the one hand, and the broad diffusion of costs coupled with large-scale tax evasion, on the other (Ferrera 1984). Although these features have paradoxically produced one of the most highly consensual models of welfare expansion in Europe, they have forced Italian reformers to view the shortcomings of this model more critically than their counterparts in the northern European countries. Since in Italy there was no heritage of the labour movement to preserve, more realistic judgements could be made as to which aspects of the welfare system were worth safeguarding, which could be changed and which objectives could and should be achieved in the current circumstances.

The point of departure is the extremely large growth of public expenditure relative to GDP, and of social expenditure within it, that has come about over the past forty years. In this, Italy has followed the same pattern as the other European countries, with the exception of its greater emphasis on money transfers as opposed to the provision of services (Ferrera 1984; Artoni and Ranci Ortigosa 1989). However, this growth has been accompanied neither by an improvement in the quality of services nor by greater clarity concerning which goals to pursue. Instead, a stream of legislative measures have been enacted which, in the pension sector for instance, have ended up producing a chaotic system combined with 'perverse effects' (Regonini 1987).

Responsibility for this situation lies mainly with the manner in which these policies have been produced and implemented. The absolute predominance of legislation, which often conceals the primacy of the political parties and of their representation of corporatist micro-interests, the weakness of the technical bureaucracies compared with their counterparts in other countries, the fragmentation of the institutional and organizational context: these are the ingredients of welfare 'Italian-style' (Dente 1985). Under these conditions the main priority in tackling the crisis of the welfare state must necessarily be to improve the rationality and efficiency of public policies. And faced with a welfare system that fails to produce equality but guarantees the privileges of the most diverse array of clienteles and social categories, the task of establishing equity criteria with which social policies must comply seems mandatory.

But reform of public intervention may prove insufficient to cope with the diversification of needs and the requirement to enhance the individual's freedom of choice. 'Once effective public management – general and uniform – has been restored to the system of basic welfare benefits and social services, it is necessary to reaffirm, equally forcefully, the principle of the state's noninterference in the voluntary social security and welfare sector (except for the general monitoring of its performance)' (Paci 1984: 322). In this context, recreating space for the market and for forms of voluntary nonprofit action is not necessarily a conservative undertaking; it is instead profoundly innovative.

Even those who acknowledge the value, both past and present, of public expenditure for redistributive purposes and to compensate for the inequalities produced by the market cannot ignore the elephantiasis and structural deficiency of the Italian public apparatus, which has commandeered all welfare functions for itself, absorbing resources without delivering services of adequate quality. The difficulty, however, lies in identifying a new point of equilibrium between public and private, a new mix between state, market and institutions based on solidarity – an equilibrium on which, moreover, the protection of citizens against social risks has always depended (Balbo 1987). And it lies, above all, in society's inability to control overall effects, namely the match between the goals pursued through the welfare system and the results actually achieved.

STATE, MARKET AND THE SOCIAL REGULATION OF THE ECONOMY

I have so far restricted my analysis to the specific features of the relationship between state and the economy in Italy. From the 'peculiarities' of the Italian case various authors have drawn the too-hasty conclusion that it cannot be handled by analytical categories developed for the purposes of comparison. In this section, I intend to show instead that if Italy is viewed from a less conventional perspective, it displays those crucial aspects of the relationship between state, society and the economy that typify the advanced industrial democracies in general – and it does so with especial clarity. In any case, whether these aspects are equally present in other countries or whether they are particularly prominent in Italy, they should be fitted into an analytical framework, not simply dismissed as eccentric.

I begin with the general question of the growth – or conversely the decline – of state regulation of the economy in the advanced industrial democracies. In the Introduction, I argued that this question is too simplistic, besides being fundamentally ill-conceived. And it appears even more misleading when one specifically analyses the Italian case. The patterns of relationships between state and the economy, in fact, vary greatly from one area of economic activity to another, and they also vary over time. During the past twenty years in Italy, there have been cases in which state intervention has increased, cases in which the type of public regulation has changed and cases in which the role of the state has declined.

In a number of areas – health, industrial policy and industrial relations – the late 1970s and early 1980s were marked by legislation and practice which brought a significant increase in state interventionism. With regard to health care, for example, 1978 saw the creation of an Italian national health service. Similarly, in 1977, a law on industrial restructuring sought to strengthen the state's role in industrial growth and to increase its instruments of intervention. With regard to industrial relations, in 1983 and 1984 the government assumed a more vigorous role in promoting concerted agreements between employers' associations and the unions.

By contrast, monetary policy underwent a series of incremental changes intended to give greater scope to market forces in the determination of interest rates, in the growth of the money supply and in other related areas (Addis 1987; Epstein and Schor 1989). And the declining role of the state, with the simultaneous growth of that of the market, certainly extended beyond monetary policies, although this was only rarely the result of explicit measures.

For example, the creation of a national health service in Italy provided numerous opportunities for the parallel growth of private medical services, and therefore intensified the role of the market and nonpublic institutions in overall health care delivery (Granaglia 1989). In social services more generally, nonstate forms of regulation – not just the market but also the family and voluntary organizations – continued to grow in importance (Paci 1989). With regard to the labour market, the 1980s saw the introduction of greater flexibility in hiring and in working hours. This gave greater scope to market relationships, although market-based regulation continued to be tempered by kinship and solidarity relations (Reyneri 1989). Finally, Italian industrial relations in the 1980s also reflected the revival and wider acceptance of the logic of the market (Cella 1989), although this resulted less from explicit policies than from the new requirements imposed by international competition and by the declining bargaining power of the unions.

Nevertheless, the Italian case demonstrates very clearly a point that I made in the Introduction: namely, that it is a mistake to regard the state and the market as the only two institutions which regulate economic activity, and even more so to maintain that they are necessarily antithetical to each other. Although in some countries this view may be to some extent appropriate, it cannot be generalized to all of them, and for three principal reasons, which the Italian case illustrates with particular clarity.

The first reason is that there is no single, universal form of public intervention in the economy. The state can, in fact, intervene in the economic system in a wide variety of ways and thereby produce a wide variety of outcomes. An important consequence of this is that profound changes may come about in the regulation of the economy even though the extent of public intervention remains the same: it is sufficient for the nature of such intervention to change.

The second reason is that state and market are not the only forms the regulation of economic activities can take. Alongside them, self-regulation by large interest organizations – that is, forms of concertation among private governments – is of increasing importance. And a major role in the regulation of economic activities continues to be played by the solidarity networks of kinship, family, clan and community. Hence, it follows that in those cases and in those periods in which the state has effectively and significantly reduced its intervention in the economy, this action has not necessarily been followed by a corresponding expansion in the room available for the market, since the role of the other above-mentioned forms of social regulation may increase.

The third reason is the following. When we examine specific areas of economic and social activity – for example, the labour market, health service, industrial relations or monetary policy – we find that state, market, private governments and solidarity networks are not always mutually exclusive; they often, in fact, interweave in complex ways. In other words, we find that each of these areas is structured by a mix of institutions, by a blend among forms of state and social regulation, and not by just one of them. I shall now examine each of these three reasons in turn and refer them to the Italian case.

1. The experience of the advanced industrial democracies in general shows that the state has a highly differentiated and articulated array of instruments with which to intervene in the economy. First of all, the state can exercise its legislative and administrative authority to determine directly the way in which a complex set of activities are co-ordinated and structured (an example in Italy being the regulation of entry to the labour market by means of the public employment offices or the disciplining of dismissals).

Second, the state may use its authority to reinforce the outcomes of other forms of regulation. This kind of intervention I call 'authority lending', by which I mean the legitimation of the ways in which a set of activities and relationships are co-ordinated by regulatory institutions other than the state (e.g., the so-called *leggi contrattate* [negotiated laws] widespread in Italy during the late 1970s, i.e., the legal ratification of agreements reached by private interest organizations).

Third, the state can use its authority to establish rules of the game which permit or constrain the operation of other forms of regulation (an example being antimonopoly legislation of the kind enacted in Italy in the early 1990s). This is indirect intervention designed only to condition the operation of the other regulatory institutions – although the success of regulation may often depend on it.

Fourth, the state may intervene indirectly to condition other forms of regulation, not by exerting its authority but by supplying economic resources (e.g., in Italy, financial incentives for the industrialization of the Mezzogiorno). Unlike the preceding case, this is purely allocative or supportive intervention (although, of course, it may at times be crucial) which provides resources in addition to those allocated by the other regulatory institutions.

The first and fourth types of intervention have always predominated in Italy. More than in other countries, the pervasive role of legislation and the 'panoply of instruments available to the state' (Cassese 1987) have increased opportunities for direct intervention in the economy. At the same time, the vulnerability of Italian public institutions to pressure from a multiplicity of interests has expanded purely allocative and supportive intervention. The indirect, conditional type of regulation typical of the Anglo-Saxon countries, by contrast, is conspicuously absent in Italy. The historical reasons for this have been brilliantly set out by Cassese (1987), to whose analysis the reader is referred.

Examination of the legislation that has accompanied economic development reveals that the Italian state is equipped with an array of instruments with which to influence the economy that very few other modern states can match. Indeed, there is no area of entrepreneurial activity in Italy not subject to some form of intervention by the public powers: from the decision to create a firm, through the raising of capital, the hiring of personnel, the allocation of investments, the fixing of product quality, to the setting of prices (Cassese 1987: 45–6). The outstanding feature of the relationship between the state and the economy in Italy is therefore the extraordinary place occupied by the former in the latter throughout the country's history. There is, however, a second feature that should be stressed: the absence in Italy of institutions which are common in other countries. Until very recently, the most striking example of this was Italy's lack of antimonopoly legislation, which is part of the more general absence in the country of general and indirect forms of regulation such as that performed by the British inspectorates or the U.S. regulatory agencies.

The reasons for this reside in the delayed beginnings of the Italian state and economy, and the consequent need for accelerated development. Italy was a latecomer country not only in the formation of the state, but also in the formation of a market and in economic development. This delay explains the urgency with which the government has sought to eliminate obstacles to growth and to guarantee a minimum of uniformity:

with the consequence that the public powers behave like an army impetuously invading enemy territory, leaving behind enclaves which are not entirely controlled or handed over to others for control by proxy. On the one hand, therefore, one has rapid and forceful state intervention. On the other, one notes the acceptance by the state of powerful private empires, with which it comes to terms. (Cassese 1987: 49)

The implication of this argument, therefore, is that a shift in the relationships between the Italian state and the economy may come about not only through the expansion or contraction of the state, which increases or reduces room for the market, but also through a change in the type of intervention in the economic system undertaken by the state itself. Tentative signs of such change have appeared in recent years: the long, drawn-out gestation of anti-monopoly legislation; the slow but irreversible privatization of state-controlled companies or banks; the labour market legislation which has eliminated numerous administrative constraints, in some cases replacing them with procedural ones. Behind these changes lies the profound crisis of the Italian political parties, which were once the principal actors and beneficiaries of traditional state intervention.

2. The second reason does not require extensive illustration. I have already argued that state and market are not the only forms that the regulation of economic activities can take, and the Italian case provides ample empirical support for this contention. First of all, various large interest organizations regulate their relationships with their members, and between these and the members of other associations, by operating as veritable private governments. In Italy, indeed, the regulation of industrial activity and of the labour market results more from agreements among large interest organizations than from state legislation or from the simple workings of the market (Chiesi and Martinelli 1989).

Second, solidarity relationships – especially those mediated through the institutions of the family, kinship and other interpersonal ties – continue to perform important social-economic functions. This is true not only of the Mezzogiorno (Catanzaro 1983; Trigilia 1992), but also of the country's areas of earlier industrialization – as Reyneri's (1988, 1989) analysis of the role of relational networks in the functioning of the labour market has demonstrated. Moreover, the extensive literature on the small-firm areas of the 'Third Italy' highlights the decisive influence of trust and subcultural relationships on economic performance (Bagnasco 1988; Trigilia 1986).

3. As I have said, examination of the ways in which specific areas of economic-social activity are effectively regulated in Italy reveals that state, market, private governments and solidarity networks – that is, the various institutions that regulate the economy – are not always mutually antithetical. That is to say, when one of them increases its range of action, the others do not necessarily lose their hitherto important functions. More frequently these forms of regulation blend together, not just in the sense that they coexist – which would be a rather trivial observation – but in the sense that they often involve mutual support rather than mutual exclusion. I shall cite a number of examples in clarification of this point.

First, there are numerous cases in Italy of what is formally state regulation but which – because of the manner in which it is implemented – allows market relationships, community ties or associative action to extend their range of influence. This interweaving is illustrated by the two following groups of examples. The first group comprises cases of extremely rigid legislation based mainly on binding and universalistic principles (of which an example was, until recently, Italian labour market legislation). This apparently rigid legislation, however, allows (one might almost say induces) numerous circumventions; that is, it leaves room for the market and community ties to operate. An example of this is the systematic circumvention by numerous firms of the public job placement service – and, in general, labour market regulations – by resorting to community networks. The second group of examples comprises those legislative or administrative provisions which merely ratify agreements reached among organized interests or norms established by private governments – thereby 'lending', so to speak, the authority of the state to such agreements or norms. This category includes the above-mentioned *leggi contrattate* between the social partners or the ministerial sanctioning of decisions reached by self-governing bodies like the Consiglio Universitario Nazionale (National University Council) or the Consiglio Nazionale della Pubblica Istruzione (National Education Council), to which public functions have been delegated.

Second, one observes numerous cases of what is apparently nonstate regulation but in which state intervention is nevertheless essential for the other regulatory institutions to function effectively. In other words, this is a form of regulation in which the state has no direct role, but which can come about only through state intervention. Examples are provided by all those situations in which activities apparently regulated by the market (like the creation or closure of firms), or by solidarity relations (e.g., services provided by voluntary organizations in the so-called third sector), or by agreements reached among associations (e.g., the agreements to alter the wage indexation mechanism) are, in fact, at least partly the result of intervention by public agencies, which allocate resources precisely in order to enable these other forms of regulation to operate. An example of the first situation is the role of incentives and financial transfers to firms (Chiesi and Martinelli 1989; Ferrera 1989); of the second, the financial support provided by the state to voluntary organizations; of the third, the compensations financed out of state funds which enable social partners to reach concerted agreements.

THE DYNAMICS OF CHANGE

Also apparently more difficult to interpret in Italy than in other advanced industrial democracies are changes in the relationships between the economy and society. Here too, however, the difficulty stems largely from the lack of an adequate analytical framework, so that attention often focuses on more superficial aspects while neglecting deeper-lying dynamics. To a lesser extent, it also stems from actual differences in the Italian case. These differences, however, should be interpreted not with instruments created ad hoc but with ones possessing more general applicability. In this section I shall concentrate on the changes that have taken place in the relationships between the economy and society in Italy from the point of view of the role of organized interests. I shall restrict myself to suggesting possible lines of interpretation: these, however, cannot be given detailed treatment in this book, which does not specifically concern the Italian case.

Those who set out to examine the relationships in Italy between organized interests, economy and society in the past twenty to twenty-five years are invariably struck by an apparent paradox. The points of departure and arrival are extremely distant from each other, yet analysis of individual phases of this longer period creates the predominant impression of inertia, of sluggishness, of resistance to change.

The Italian trade unions, for instance, at the beginning of the 1970s were undoubtedly the most militant and adversarial of all the unions in the advanced industrial countries; and they were for a long time thereafter accused of stubborn resistance to change. Today, by contrast, the Italian unions are among the most receptive in Europe to consensual solutions to the problem of industrial adjustment (see Chapter 8). The figures on Italian economic performance arouse the same reaction among observers: How can it be that in the 1970s Italy was the Cinderella of Europe (indeed, according to a former U.S. ambassador to Italy, 'the European Bangladesh'), but in the 1980s a worldwide success story, even though many authors continued to stress the failure of every attempt at innovation in the country?

Of course, the first and easiest reply is to divide the period into different phases and then to seek an explanation of how the passage from one to another came about.[1] With regard to the relationships between organized interests, economy and society, various models have been developed (or imported) to capture the characteristic features of these phases. One finds, in fact, three distinct models which fit best with three different phases.

Thus, the late 1960s and early 1970s are by now generally considered to have been the period of 'social mobilization' and the building of 'collective identities' (Pizzorno et al. 1978; Tarrow 1990). The second half of the 1970s and the beginning of the 1980s are generally viewed as the phase of political exchange and neocorporatist attempts (Regini 1982, 1987). And although agreement among commentators increasingly diminishes the closer one approaches the present, it seems clear that the late 1980s and early 1990s were dominated by flexibility and diversification (Regini and Sabel 1989). Collective mobilization, political exchange and flexibility are therefore three concepts which – despite the ambiguities left unresolved, indeed reinforced, by the interminable terminological disputes that have accompanied their development – are still used to encapsulate the principal features of each of these three phases. They are concepts, moreover, useful for comparative analysis because they can be applied to various national contexts. There still remains the suspicion, however, that they may obscure the co-presence of different elements in each phase, and therefore the relative continuity of change.

First of all, these three models reflect the predominance of different actors in each phase, and their succession is often viewed as resulting from changes in power relationships or in each actor's function. From this point of view, of decisive importance in the first phase is the power of workers and unions, in the second the increased role of the state and in the third the revival of employer initiative and hegemony. These changed power relationships reflect, in turn, profound changes in the Italian economic, political and social context.

However, this line of analysis has emphasized certain contextual factors in each phase at the expense of others. Regarding the first phase, attention has focused mainly on changes in the composition, features and culture of the labour force (the emergence of 'mass-workers'; Accornero 1981). Regarding the second, priority has been given to changes in the state's regulation of economic activities (the growth and crisis of the Keynesian welfare state; Bordogna and Provasi 1984). Analysis of the third phase has concentrated on changes in the organization of production and of the labour market (the end of Fordism; Regini and Sabel 1989). Each of these factors, however, has played an important role in the overall process of change, a role which has not been restricted to one particular phase. If we are to develop a more complex and more coherent explanatory framework, therefore, we must redress the balance among these factors while bearing in mind other, equally important contextual features.

Second, these three models capture three separate occasions on which certain features have apparently predominated. By generalizing these features to an entire period, while neglecting others, these models stress the inner coherences of each phase and the differences between one phase and another. But how can one account for such abrupt and dramatic changes between one model and another in a context like Italy, where, as we know, changes have been slow and incremental (Lange and Regini 1989)? To return to the question I asked earlier, how can there be such a radical difference between the beginning and end of the past quarter of a century when, within each intermediate phase, the prevalent impression is one of inertia?

Evidently, many of the features of the analytical model proposed to capture a new phase were already present in its predecessor. This poses the problem of providing a better account of the slow gestation and the equally slow disappearance of those features assumed to be characteristic of each phase. Is it the everyday observer who fails to notice what is slowly changing and growing new shoots? Or is it the analyst of turning-points who distorts the vision of change by introducing categories which exaggerate the differences between one phase and another? Or, and this is more likely, are both of them the villains of the story? These are extremely important questions, and students of the Italian case and its change should bear them more closely in mind before they reach hasty conclusions about anomalies which partly depend on the observer's standpoint.

If the continuity of history – as opposed to the discontinuity of the models developed to explain it – raises the problem of how to conduct comparisons over time, it is equally true that there are diversities in the history of the advanced industrial countries which are often overlooked by excessively uniform analytical models. And here the problem of international comparisons arises. From this point of view, Italy has passed through the same phases as other European countries in the past twenty-five years, but with two important differences. First, the social mobilization of the late 1960s in Italy was particularly intense and long-lasting, so that the breakdown of economic and social equilibria in the country was more profound and had more enduring effects. Second, and more important, in other European countries changes in the context (i.e., in the organization of production, in the state's regulation of economic activities and in the composition, features and culture of the labour force) have been slower and steadier and have taken place over longer periods of time. In Italy, by contrast, there have been sudden accelerations in the process, so that each phase in the relationship between organized interests, economy and society has not had time to establish itself fully before the next phase begins.

Although, for the purposes of comparison, study of the Italian case must continue to use models consistent with those employed to analyse other advanced industrial countries, perhaps here resides one of the principal reasons for the discomfiture mentioned at the beginning of this chapter: the mounting unease as one realizes that Italy is always 'a little different', that Italian reality is always more multifaceted and multiform, that the situation of the country is more complicated than the models used to interpret it. Each phase (except for the mobilization phase) seems more unstable and provisional. Consequently, interpretative models are apparently less clear, less generally applicable and less able to yield unequivocal results in Italy than they are in the other countries with which comparisons are made.

An example is provided by the analytical dichotomies of conflict/co-operation or centralization/decentralization frequently used to analyse the evolution of Italian industrial relations. As several studies have shown, even in the relatively co-operative and centralized phase of political exchange in the late 1970s, conflicts continued to arise in Italy, as did bargaining at the peripheral level (Golden 1988). Yet we also know that in the next phase, which was marked by renewed tension at the central level, in many Italian companies the joint management of restructuring developed instead (see Chapter 8).

This prompts one to ask whether it is not precisely the above-mentioned pattern of sudden accelerations and discontinuities that has created an underlying or even underground level of relationships between organized interests, economy and society – a level at which behaviour is the reverse of that suggested by the dominant model. Perhaps these fits and starts have been responsible for the asynchronous behaviour, the delays and the premature beginnings, the long waves that have continued to propagate themselves even when the wind has turned. On this basis, perhaps, one could devise a comparative theoretical framework which accommodates even the peculiarities and the anomalies of the Italian case – analytical categories which would otherwise be unacceptable to the social scientist.

The micro-social regulation of economic adjustment

In Part I we saw how the model of the concerted and centralized political regulation of the economy, after functioning with conspicuous success for almost fifty years, entered a phase of decline. This is by no means a novel finding – indeed, it is taken for granted by that strand of debate in the social sciences which, by paraphrasing the title of an article by Panitch (1980), we could call 'the crisis industry' – but it should be viewed in a new light when set in relation to the tendencies that I shall now examine in Part II.

To begin with, the emphasis should be placed on these three adjectives – political, concerted and centralized – as applied to the model of economic regulation described in preceding chapters. The fact that three distinct adjectives are required to specify this type of regulation demonstrates that there is not just a single nonmarket institution by which the economy can be regulated, or a single way in which nonmarket institutions work. This was the principal error of the many analyses conducted during the 1980s of the deregulation of Western economies, analyses which often did nothing more than simplistically echo what, for business people and neo-laissez-faire politicians, was a slogan from the realm of wishful thinking. But, on closer examination, even considerably more sophisticated analyses of the advent of 'disorganized capitalism' (Offe 1985; Lash and Urry 1987) were based on a similar premise: that the crisis of a historically specific form of regulation signalled the decline *tout court* in the capacity of social and political institutions to structure economic behaviour.

Instead, as I pointed out in the Preface and as will emerge more clearly in the following chapters, the economic adjustment of the 1980s was by no means based, everywhere, on a straightforward return to the 'free operation of the market'. Indeed, in several European countries it was helped by the existence of institutionally dense situations, which shaped actors' strategies and therefore the ways in which these countries' economies were restructured.

The changes that occurred during the 1980s made the ability of firms to become more flexible and to diversify crucial for the performances of the respective national economies (see Chapter 6) and overshadowed the role played by public policies. Consequently, the economic system's centre of gravity (as well as the attention of scholars) shifted from the level of macro-political management to the micro-level of firms' behaviour. The state relinquished its role as the key actor in economic processes to the entrepreneur, who was the indubitable protagonist of adjustment during the 1980s. From macro-political, the regulation of economic activities became prevalently micro-social. Solidarity networks regained the importance they had apparently lost in orienting economic behaviour (Granovetter 1985; Reyneri 1988), while industrial relations institutions structured the strategies and concrete choices of actors within the firm (Pontusson 1992). An institutionally regulated economy, therefore, was not succeeded by a deregulated one; only the modes of regulation and the most important institutions changed.

Nor was the final characteristic of political regulation, that of being substantially concerted with organized interests, radically contradicted by the emergence of micro-social regulation. Despite predictions to the contrary, forms of more or less institutionalized consensus within the firm came to represent, in many cases, a functional substitute for the macro-national concertation now in progressive decline. This point appears so crucial for the emerging forms of micro-social regulation to acquire the stability and significance of a model that my following analysis begins with it.

5

The crisis of political exchange and the growth of micro-concertation

In this chapter I describe the simultaneous occurrence of two phenomena which, in the 1980s, characterized the role of organized interests in the economies of several European countries. Because these phenomena have usually been analysed separately, it has proved difficult to capture their overall dynamics. Inevitably, therefore, any conclusion concerning their impact has been at best partial.

On the one hand, the traditional form of social concertation as practised in Europe in the 1970s and early 1980s – that is, macro-concertation at a national level – is now everywhere in decline. The general reasons for the structural instability of systematic political exchange, in whatever form, were discussed in Chapter 2. But what were the specific features of the kind of concertation which was practised in Europe in those years and which today faces severe difficulties?

First, this form of bargaining was strongly political, not so much because of the frequent involvement of the government in formally tripartite negotiation, as because its symbolic function was to exchange legitimation between the government itself and the social partners. Second, this political exchange was highly centralized, both in the sense that it took place at the central (i.e., national) level and in the sense that it was the central component of the industrial relations system. National-level concertation was the pivot around which all inter-actor relationships rotated, and company-level bargaining and other forms of decentralized relationship were subordinate to it. Third, this was largely institutionalized bargaining, to the point that in many cases attempts were made to convert it to periodic formal agreements. Fourth, in this kind of concertation, problems were defined in an all-inclusive and aggregate manner, and the solutions to them were similarly framed. The containment of overall labour costs was regarded as the crucial problem, and the compensations to the social partners willing to pursue this goal were conceived in equally aggregate terms: labour market measures to foster employment, fiscal policies favouring firms and so forth. In short, all of these four features largely lost their significance in the 1980s, and thus this kind of concertation entered everywhere into critical decline.

Yet, before discussing the reasons for this decline, I must point out (in order to avoid an overly partial account of reality) that these years also saw the simultaneous emergence of new forms and new levels of concertation. In other words, the decline of concertation at the macro-national level did not, in general, lead to a crisis *tout court* in the joint regulation of work – as has been frequently maintained (or predicted).

Instead, in various European countries during the 1980s there emerged new forms of micro-concertation designed to encourage industrial adjustment. These were forms of concertation at the company level, and sometimes at the territorial or sectoral level as well, which translated into a common acceptance of goals, constraints and compatibilities, an acceptance which could not be entirely accounted for by changes in power relationships to labour's disadvantage. Compared with traditional concertation, which was an attempt at the joint management of inflation, these new forms may be called 'the concertation of industrial adjustment': the process that enables companies to restructure and to (re)acquire competitiveness.

THE DECLINE OF MACRO-NATIONAL CONCERTATION

In the second half of the 1970s, as we know, in various European countries concertation between state, unions and employers' associations was assigned a key role in fostering the revival of economic growth. This was because the nature of the problems then considered to be crucial made this particular form of bargaining necessary.

Governments regarded the concertation of incomes policies as essential if inflation was to be brought under control and if the conflict then widespread in various sectors of society was to be regulated – especially in those contexts where the trade unions were still viewed primarily as viable instruments for aggregating consensus. Most employers, on the other hand, considered concertation to be a second-best solution, and for a similar reason: even if the unions had been weakened by the recession, in many European countries they were still strong enough to obstruct the return to a nonregulated market.

Finally, although the unions themselves were often internally divided over the degree of centrality to be given to concertation, they saw it as a viable instrument with which to control those economic phenomena – which partly stemmed from their own previous actions – most damaging to workers (recession and growing unemployment, industrial restructuring, the rising cost of living) and also as a way to compensate for their diminishing market power by acquiring institutional functions and political recognition.

In various European countries, therefore, a phase began in which major efforts were made to reach social pacts which would generate growth while at the same time cushion its most damaging effects. Nonetheless, the fact that this type of concertation has for some time been in decline, if not in deep crisis, need not be enlarged upon. It is only necessary to look at press reports and political debate in recent years to realize that, in the European countries, not only are large-scale tripartite agreements no longer stipulated but there is a general lack of interest in their analysis.[1]

Paradoxically, attempts at macro-concertation continued in the 1980s at the supranational level, precisely when this type of arrangement was so obviously in crisis in the European member countries. The European Community, in fact, tenaciously persisted in its efforts to create a 'Euro-corporatism' partly modelled on the national examples that had seemed most successful during the 1970s. To this end, it encouraged the formation of supranational interest associations and established the procedures for recognizing their status. Each of the European Community Directorates surrounded itself with a constellation of consultative committees based more on the representation of functional interests than on territorial representation. Various tripartite conferences were convened to discuss economic and social policy issues. And after 1984, action was taken to promote a 'European social dialogue' involving organized interests.

This attempt to create some sort of Europe-wide concertation also ran into difficulties, mainly because of the scant interest in it shown by employers' associations – when they were not overtly hostile. Although it has been revived in discussions on the 'social dimension' of the single market, one can confidently say that the institutions of concertation, which are everywhere in crisis at the national level, have not been re-created at the supranational one.

The immediate causes of the decline of macro-national concertation lay in the altered convenience of concertation to each of the three subjects involved; that is to say, the cost–benefit calculation of each of them changed over time. In the 1980s, governments had less need of the support of unions, given that their capacity to aggregate consensus and to legitimate government action had diminished (Carrieri and Donolo 1986). Employers, for their part, in the situation of more favourable power relationships and of the predominant market ideology of those years, now tended to regard concertation as setting unnecessary constraints on their freedom of action (Streeck 1984). Many companies, moreover, seemed to give less importance to curbing wage increases in aggregate terms – which was typically the object of traditional political exchange – and instead sought opportunities to deploy their internal work-forces more flexibly. Finally, many trade unions identified the cause of the representation crisis that hit them in the 1980s as the excessive isolation from the work-place imposed on them by centralized concertation. Even when the unions preserved a certain amount of power, therefore, their attention tended to shift away from political bargaining to the plant level, in order to rebuild their now-deteriorating relations with the rank and file.

For different reasons, therefore, all three actors involved in macro-national concertation came to regard this instrument of labour regulation and public policy-making as no longer the most viable one (or at most as a second-best solution). More specifically, as I have said, it was the weakening of the trade unions during the 1980s that altered the range of strategic benefits available to each actor. This diminished influence of the unions was matched by the relatively greater capacity of other interest groups and social movements to apply pressure. Certainly, in no European country did these actors acquire a political importance comparable with that of the 'producers' groups'; yet despite the predictions of neocorporatist theoreticians, we today find a greater plurality of old and new mechanisms for the intermediation of interests. And in this situation it is more difficult for the unions to claim the distinct or superior status that, during the period of concertation, was warranted by their ability to represent a wide spectrum of interests and social groups.

Thus, for different reasons, the European unions lost not only market and organizational power but also the 'oligopolistic position in political bargaining' with governments (Regini 1984) that they enjoyed in the late 1970s. At the same time the political representation of workers' interests apparently became more problematic. First, in many countries this representation was reappropriated by political parties. Second, it was often divided among several institutions which functioned as 'policy communities' (Richardson 1982) segmented into areas of competence (tripartite or multipartite administrative bodies for employment, training and so on). In these institutions, union representatives or experts were not necessarily accorded special status; nor did they pursue general strategies, but tended instead to behave as one actor among many. That is to say, they found themselves subject to the same constraints and the same organizational dynamics as the others.

It is possible, however, to object to my analysis of the factors responsible for the decline of macro-concertation on the grounds that they were part of a cycle which in recent years has exhausted itself. If these were not structural factors but contingent ones, the cost–benefit calculation of each actor may change once again, and macro-national concertation, with the characteristics outlined earlier, could move back towards the top of the political agenda. This objection is certainly not a minor one, and a return to some form of concertation and formal incomes policy is doubtlessly possible – as the 1993 tripartite agreement in Italy has shown. Yet it is extremely unlikely that it could once again assume the features which, as I argued at the beginning of this chapter, were responsible for its decline.

Apart from the changing cost–benefit analyses of the actors involved, in fact, there are two, more structural reasons (to which I give more extensive treatment in the next chapter) why this should be so. These reasons relate to epoch-making changes in modes of production and in the social structure which are presently eroding – probably permanently – the centrality of macro-national concertation of the kind described in the strategy of the social partners. First, the increasing diversification of the industrial relations strategies pursued both by firms and by unions – which is matched by growing diversification in the industrial fabric and the labour market – means that uniform rules produced at the national level have become increasingly ineffective. Second, the emergence of flexibility, and the greater importance attached to it by both firms and unions, compared with the traditional issues of wages and labour costs, have boosted the importance of labour regulation at the company and local levels relative to the centralized national one.

The diversification of industrial relations at the company level

That both company and union strategies diversify according to context is certainly not a novel observation. But today one witnesses the emergence of two phenomena which are to a large extent unprecedented.

1. The pre-eminence of the so-called Fordist firm (i.e., the firm based on the mass production of standard goods in large production units) has been superseded by the increasing diversification of the organization of production and work. Alongside Fordist firms, of growing importance are production systems possessing a variety of features ranging from 'flexible specialization' (Piore and Sabel 1984) to 'flexible mass production' (Boyer 1986) to 'diversified quality production' (Streeck 1992).

The organization of the Fordist factory was based on a system of rules which applied in a relatively uniform manner to all productive units and to all work relationships. Its corresponding system of industrial relations consisted, in practice, of bargaining over these rules according to equally uniform and standardized criteria, or of setting the price for their acceptance. Today, depending on the path followed by the individual firm to a post-Fordist system of production, this uniformity fades and company strategies diversify.

Of course, not all firms have restructured their production and reorganized their work-forces along post-Fordist lines. Many firms may be highly innovative technologically, but nonetheless install relatively rigid machinery. Others may redefine their relationships with suppliers and diversify production, but still adhere to the traditional Taylorist system of work organization.

Moreover, although the organization of work and personnel management may have changed profoundly for some groups of workers, it has not done so for others. The important study by Kern and Schumann (1984) of several sectors of German industry shows, for example, that restructuring often creates an élite of highly skilled workers for whom the company introduces quality circles, incentives, teamwork and direct co-operation-based relations. This élite, however, is flanked by other categories of workers who pay the price of restructuring and for whom work organization has changed not at all.

Hence, the new developments outlined earlier do not represent a uniform trend among all companies; instead, they fragment and diversify the industrial fabric and strategies pursued by employers. Moreover, the personnel policies adopted by individual companies do not apply equally to all categories of the work-force. As a consequence, the production of uniform rules at the central-national level to regulate wages, working hours, mobility or labour market entry are regarded by companies as increasingly less appropriate to their problems.

2. The unions, too, are confronted by a growing number of factors which force them to diversify their strategies. One must remember that trade-union power expanded and consolidated during a period in which the working and living conditions of the majority of wage-earners were relatively homogeneous. This situation led, in turn, to notable political homogeneity, and it enabled subcultures with strong ideological identities to flourish. It was therefore quite natural and straightforward, for the European trade unions at least, to represent in aggregate fashion interests that were already relatively homogeneous and to elaborate bargaining policies based on egalitarian and solidaristic principles.

Today, however, there is no doubt that labour has become more highly diversified. This is more than just a matter of the widening divide between a highly skilled élite and the unskilled mass that I mentioned earlier, or of the heterogeneity of occupational roles produced by the decline of the Fordist model. Also, the life-styles and personal needs of workers have diversified. And the centrality of work in people's lives has undergone, according to several surveys, major changes. It is quite reasonable to assume, therefore, that the functions assigned by workers to their unions have also altered and diversified as a result of these processes. Hence, for workers too, uniform rules produced at the national level appear increasingly less appropriate to their situation.

The central importance of flexibility

Flexibility is now a key element in the organization of production, and greater work flexibility, in particular, has become vitally important to firms. In several countries, firms at first relied on external or numerical forms of flexibility (i.e., workers entering or leaving the labour market). Soon, however, the problem arose of internal or functional flexibility and with it the central importance of quality, of a skills endowment distributed efficiently and flexibly among renewed production processes and of the speed of human intervention on machinery. These themes became the typical subjects of the workplace-based de facto co-operation described in the next section, precisely because it was impossible to handle them at the macro-national level.

The attempt of firms to place flexibility at the centre of company-level industrial relations is well known, and in the light of the many studies of the topic, it can be largely taken for granted. But interest in making working hours and work performance more flexible grew markedly among large groups of workers as well (Accornero 1988), so that the unions not infrequently found themselves under pressure from two directions – companies, on the one hand, and workers, on the other – to relax rules regarded as too rigid, standardized and uniform. Flexibility has consequently become a key focus of company industrial relations, not just because it is a major company objective but because around it pivot many of the demands advanced by a labour force which, in this respect too, has grown more diversified. And, as I have said, the centrality of flexibility has increased the importance of work regulation at the company level compared with that imposed at the centralized, political one.

THE EMERGENCE OF NEW FORMS OF CONCERTATION

So macro-concertation is everywhere in decline because of the factors outlined in the preceding section. Nonetheless, the other side of the coin is that new forms of concertation have arisen in several European countries. Only in a few national or sectoral cases have the regaining of the initiative by employers, the decline of macro-national concertation and the shift in the centre of gravity of inter-actor relations to the micro-level led to extended deregulation.

In some countries and sectors, of course, firms have taken advantage of the weaker unions by attempting to reassert the unilateral regulation of the labour force. Or they have attempted to create forms of 'human resource management' which individualize management's relations with workers and bypass collective representation by the unions. In countries like Spain, for instance, where traditional Fordist industry is still widespread and the unions are weak, the crisis of social concertation – which played such a major part in the country's economic boom after Franco – also brought a major cutback in the role of the unions (Miguelez and Prieto 1991).

But in other countries – especially Germany and Italy – the shift of initiative to the company level has brought to the fore various forms of micro-concertation based on pragmatic acknowledgement by the unions that companies must restructure if they are to compete in more difficult and volatile international markets, and on the willingness by managements to use the existing institutions of industrial relations for this purpose, rather than work against them. The German case probably comes as no surprise in this regard. But in Italy as well various studies have shown that in the 1980s trade unions were involved in many of the decisions taken at the company micro-level (see Chapter 8). In many companies, the industrial restructuring of the early 1980s was not carried forward in open conflict with the unions. Instead, it took the form of ongoing consultation, of sorts, over possible solutions to problems as and when they arose: whether to draw on the Wages Guarantee Fund or to introduce early retirement or to resort to other measures in order to handle so-called occupational surpluses; how to control the effects of technological innovation; whether to pay overtime or adopt forms of compensatory rest; and so on.

In the course of this long and stable interaction process, the unions have passed from traditional rhetoric to more concrete measures in defence of workers' interests. And many employers have come to realize that although the presence in their companies of a strong trade union willing to bargain may entail higher costs and more stringent constraints in the short period, the long-run advantage is that shop-floor reactions to management decisions are easier to predict. The reduction of uncertainty thus made possible is of major importance in a situation of highly volatile markets – a situation, that is, in which production must be constantly reorganized to meet the challenges of international competition.

This micro-concertation led to a considerable increase in the flexibility of work rules – albeit without their formal redefinition – and often to the outright joint management of industrial restructuring, although rarely to the explicit sharing of responsibility. Hence, in Chapter 8, I use the terms 'local' and 'secluded' to describe the kind of micro-concertation that has spread among many large firms and which has always been typical of the majority of small ones.

It is difficult to find clear-cut indicators of this tendency, precisely because these strategies are not ones of explicit co-operation. Nevertheless, a panel study in Italy of nearly two hundred firms (Regalia and Ronchi 1988, 1989, 1990) furnishes some quite significant findings. For example, in almost half the small firms in the sample, in three-quarters of the medium-sized ones and in around 80 per cent of the large ones, company managements regularly informed the unions about the economic and employment situation of the company. And more important from our point of view here, when company managements had to decide on a series of recurrent issues, ranging from overtime to holidays, to internal mobility, to vocational training, to technological-organizational problems, many of them involved workers' representatives in the decision-making process. The most striking finding, however, was the tendency of both firms and unions to define problems jointly, to search for mutually advantageous solutions and to make pragmatic adjustments to the needs of the other party.

Studies by Streeck (1984), Terry (1985) and other researchers have shown the existence of similar processes in German and British firms. Equally interesting is the fact that in countries of weak trade unionism like France, various companies view this weakness as hampering the type of production that emphasizes quality and rapid adaptation to the volatility of markets. Indeed, cases have been reported where companies have deliberately encouraged the formation or strengthening of workers' representative bodies so to constitute a reliable and truly representative opponent at the bargaining table – one, therefore, very different from the old 'yellow' (pro-employer) trade unions.

Why do I propose to call this phenomenon, which has now emerged in several European countries, 'micro-concertation', instead of viewing it as part of the traditional bargaining system, or perhaps as an embryonic form of co-determination? First, because this is not a matter of straightforward bargaining, in which each actor seeks to maximize its own interests and then accepts an agreement which represents a compromise among these partisan interests but which does not necessarily take account of more general or systemic constraints. Often, no formal agreement is reached in the new situation, but a relationship is created which, as in traditional concertation, presupposes the existence of shared goals or constraints.

Second, this micro-concertation differs from co-determination because, even though public institutions are not formally involved, they have assumed an important role in the process. One can easily show that nowhere have tripartite agreements (i.e., those in which the public institutions are formally present) developed at either the company or the local level. Nevertheless, public institutions often play a decisive indirect role in enabling the emergence of the relationships that I have described.

For example, the de facto participation of unions in the management of external flexibility – that is, exit from the labour market – would have been unthinkable without the action taken by the governments of many countries in granting early retirement or employment subsidies to facilitate the process. At the peripheral level, the resources provided by local institutions and governments have frequently been even more important in promoting what I earlier called the micro-concertation of industrial adjustment. A number of relevant examples are provided by research conducted in Italy (Regini and Sabel 1989): the use in the Prato area of social services to make highly flexible working hours possible or the creation in Modena of a Business Centre which provides marketing and technical consultation services for small firms in the area (see Chapter 8).

One should also remember that the public powers were not always formal participants is traditional macro-national concertation either. In many cases, in fact, they acted as the 'incubator' for agreements among social partners. This, for example, was the experience of Sweden – one of the countries where concertation was the most stable and pervasive – and of Germany during the period of *Konzertierte Aktion*. Apart from terminological considerations, however, what matters is that these forms of micro-concertation somewhat unexpectedly became central to inter-actor relationships, and they were one of the principal factors responsible for the renewed competitiveness of European industry during the 1980s.

One may well ask why macro-national social concertation was so widely regarded in the 1970s as the only possible option for countries in acute economic crisis or affected by severe political instability (Great Britain, Italy, Spain). Theoretically, there were at least three institutional strategies with which these problems could have been confronted on a consensual basis. The first was institutionalized political exchange itself, or the tripartite concertation of economic policies. The second was the use of centralized bilateral accords to handle these problems, without the intervention of the government. The third option was to encourage some form of co-determination, or the joint management of the most urgent problems at the company level. As we know, in the late 1970s and early 1980s, after the brief experimentation of some countries with the second strategy, it was the first that came to predominate. The third option was never taken up, nor indeed was it even seriously considered. Why not?

The reasons are numerous. The most significant of them relate to the nature of the problems (inflation, and therefore the cost of labour) prioritized by the political and economic agendas of all countries. They also relate to the extent to which governments in those years were willing to guarantee agreements and to compensate for the costs incurred by the social partners, and to the extent to which the latter were willing to allow governments to perform this role. There is also, however, a more cultural reason, one which is of major importance in explaining the strategy that then prevailed: the general belief (i.e., the belief shared by all three actors) that responsible behaviour at the company level was unattainable because the workers' representative bodies were, apparently, too vulnerable to what would presumably be radical demands by the rank and file. It was therefore widely believed that the central unions – accustomed as they were to representing general interests and to allowing little room for sectoral ones – could be involved in a logic of political exchange – not, however, the peripheral representative bodies, because these would probably adopt a markedly antagonistic stance.

Although there was perhaps some justification for this view in the late 1970s, it was never thereafter seriously questioned, even though profound changes had occurred in production sites in the meantime. Thus, only much later, in the second half of the 1980s, did the realization dawn that matters had developed in a manner very different from what had been predicted. That is to say, whereas attempts at macro-national concertation had everywhere either encountered major difficulties or failed, in the more sheltered arenas of firms and certain geographical areas the micro-concertation I have described had gradually and spontaneously come into being.

These events occurred in the 1980s, but various developments since then induce one to believe that the future of relationships among producers' groups also lies more in micro- than in macro-concertation, mainly because many employers now find this alternative increasingly attractive. Indeed, several companies which used to regard restructuring as only a temporary phase now envisage scenarios in which – given the continuing turmoil of markets – adjustment is a constant strategic requirement. It seems generally more advantageous in these scenarios to concert decisions with unions which now impose lower costs and weaker constraints than they did in the past and which in return legitimate entrepreneurial decisions vis-à-vis the government and workers.

In fact, although many firms have fully regained the initiative, they still believe it necessary to mobilize all the resources available to them, including internal resources and workers' consensus. If there is one lesson that employers have learned from the long phase of restructuring, it is that the industrial relations system is often a resource because it is part of the repertoire of rules and procedures that the firm can deploy to cope with uncertainty; it is not merely an obstacle to adjustment.

Yet there is another key reason why, in the 1980s, the micro-concertation of flexibility and the co-management of restructuring came to predominate. This was the growing awareness among workers that firms had adopted a dynamic posture which contrasted with the inertia and short-sightedness of the unions. Although frequently tough and aggressive, this posture nevertheless offered a way out of the crisis. In other words, managerial culture has slowly regained a certain hegemony over the culture of collective defence, often rigid and standardized and indifferent to the needs of the firm. And the fact that many workers are now beginning to regard flexibility as synonymous with dynamism, while the more traditional positions in some cases still taken up by the unions seem counterproductive and ill-suited to their needs, will probably help to stabilize the role of micro-concertation, extending it beyond the simple management of phases of crisis and restructuring.

A BRIEF CONCLUSION

The conclusions of this chapter are, I believe, largely implicit in the analysis conducted so far. They can, in fact, be summed up in a single sentence. Traditional macro-national concertation may still have a future – but only if change comes about in the four features that I described at the beginning of this chapter. However, analysts should now direct their attention more towards the new forms of micro- and meso-concertation (i.e., those at the company and local level), since it is here that the new nucleus of the industrial relations system is located, and it is here that the most important conditions for the future vitality of the industrial system are to be found.

Of the four features of traditional concertation, two are ever-present and probably risky temptations: (a) making macro-national concertation the level of relationship to which collective bargaining and in particular company-level bargaining are subordinate; (b) assigning it wholly aggregate contents, such as the containment of labour costs or labour policies, which ignore the requirements of flexibility and local adjustments.

Of course, whenever the international economy shows signs of recovery, governments and employers begin once again to believe that the concertation of certain decisions with central labour representatives – that is, those more sensitive to the economic compatibility of their claims – is to their advantage. For the unions as well, the lesson to be learned from the failures of the recent past is that not every form of political exchange should be rejected out of hand.

It is likely, however, that all the actors who have undergone this long learning process will agree that they have learned one overriding lesson: namely, that concertation should be relieved of the expectations and overburdensome tasks assigned to it in the late 1970s and early 1980s. Certain lighter but crucial functions must be specified for macro-national concertation to fulfil, while support should simultaneously be given to that micro- and meso-concertation which arose spontaneously during the 1980s and which today perhaps requires some form of institutionalization.

6

The search for flexibility

By now, the observation that firms and trade unions today face markets that are much more volatile than they used to be has become largely a commonplace.[1] Almost equally commonplace is the view that, in order to react to this greater volatility, a growing number of firms have been obliged to abandon, or at least to alter substantially, their productive and organizational strategies (in particular, the mass production of standard goods by means of specialized and rigid machinery operated by semiskilled workers) – strategies which presupposed stability. For these firms, adjustment to changed economic conditions has entailed first and foremost increased flexibility – that is, the ability to use machines and workers in different combinations in order to adapt to changing market conditions. Unions, too, have had to adjust, and they have sometimes discovered in the process that participation in the management of flexibility offers them new opportunities to regain the institutional authority over workers that they had lost.

FLEXIBILITY AND DIVERSIFICATION

Indeed, the breakup of mass markets and constant shifts in the level and composition of demand are general, almost universal, phenomena today. The assertion that firms must cope with more volatile markets is, as I have said, by now a commonplace and one widespread in the business literature. One might even say that there is a broad consensus that it is now impossible to forecast demand by means of market research. The successes or failures of new products are today practically the only available indicators of what the market can absorb.

This increased market volatility has forced large firms to question seriously the cardinal principle of mass production: namely, the separation of conception and execution (Piore and Sabel 1984). The efficiency of mass production depended on economies of scale, and to obtain economies of scale it is necessary to subdivide work into a series of highly specialized operations, some of which can be mechanized while others are performed by semiskilled workers. In order to reorganize production along these lines, it is by definition necessary to separate the conception of production from its execution.

However, this division between conception and execution made sense only as long as the enormous costs of maintaining complex organizations to plan and control the division of labour, as well as the investments in special-purpose or product-specific machines which these organizations required, could be amortized over large-scale production runs.

But the more markets fragmented during the 1970s, the more this proved difficult. A profound revision of the criteria of company organization based on some sort of reintegration between conception and execution therefore became necessary. This was the paramount problem for firms in the 1980s. And on the greater or lesser ability to find satisfactory solutions depended the degree of success achieved by adjustment processes in the various national economies.

However, this break with the old models of organization has not automatically led to the dominance and diffusion of a single alternative. Although an increasing number of firms are aware that their survival depends on greater flexibility, there is no common agreement among them over an alternative model of flexibility. In areas such as the organization of subcontracting or the distribution of authority and responsibilities between corporate headquarters and operating units, there seems to be some convergence of views on new and more flexible organizational models to adopt. But there is no such clear convergence regarding the use of technology, the organization of work, personnel management and industrial relations.

In part, these divergent responses to the common problem of adapting to market volatility simply reflect the confusion of any period of transition (Streeck 1987). For example, even firms operating in the same sector may well disagree over their estimates of the long-term level of market volatility. And the widespread view that all predictions in this regard are uncertain induces firms to hedge their bets – which they do by pursuing a range of strategies, by steering a middle course between what appear to be too radical alternatives or by ensuring their continuing capacity to switch back to old models.

Apart from such uncertainties, however, this diversity of the flexibility strategies reflects the multiplicity of the means by which the goal of flexibility can be achieved. Mass-production systems, too, used to differ greatly – in their organization of industrial relations, for example – although they employed similar technologies. Similarly, one productive system may be more flexible than another in many respects but not necessarily in all. For instance, a flexible subcontracting system may induce a large firm to use relatively inflexible capital goods or work practices. This signifies that elements of new models of flexible production systems coexist in practice with elements from older rigidity-based models.

The uncertainty of firms' reactions to new market conditions becomes even more apparent if we consider their strategies of personnel management and industrial relations (see Chapter 7). The relationship between firms' choices in this field and those in other areas of strategic importance for them is even less clear-cut. The problem is not that industrial relations have remained unchanged since the 1970s; nor can one say that changes in industrial relations contradict the principles guiding the redistribution of decision-making roles in the firm or the redefinition of subcontracting relations. In almost all countries, in fact, one observes a tendency to decentralize authority in order to increase firms' capacity for local adjustment to changing external conditions. The problem is rather that the direction of change in personnel and industrial relations policies is influenced by other factors, ones which relate to the trade-union tradition and to the institutional and cultural features of an area or a company. To a certain extent, this has always been the case. But the decline of the hegemonic (i.e., Fordist) model of the organization of production and labour relations, and the greater uncertainty consequent upon it, has given more weight to local factors (Locke 1994) – that is, specific company and geographical characteristics – in conditioning the management of human resources and industrial relations.

In spite of management uncertainties, the one requirement that this new industrial organization entails for workers is their much greater flexibility – in the sense of adaptability to different tasks, mobility from one job to another, willingness to work more when orders must be met and less when production stagnates and an ability to react to the unexpected so that product quality can be maintained.

THE CONSEQUENCES OF THE SEARCH FOR FLEXIBILITY

Since the influential book by Piore and Sabel (1984) was published, there has been a growing literature on the decline of Fordism as a system based on mass production and mass consumption. The 'Fordist wage relationship' has also been analysed by the French economists at Cepremap (see, e.g., Boyer 1986) as the mode of regulation dominant in the capitalist system until the 1970s. Here, however, I am interested solely in the consequences of a particular form of the organization of production on work and industrial relations. From this point of view, Fordism was typified by the following: the dominance of large companies committed to mass production; the growth of the semiskilled worker, who became the dominant figure on the factory floor, superseding the previous dualism between the skilled and the unskilled worker; the greater emphasis of employers on the overall organization of the work process inside the firm rather than on the individual worker's performance.

The effects of the Fordist model on industrial relations were quite evident. Large masses of workers, with similar interests and hegemonic occupational groups, were concentrated into big production units. Trade unions based their power on these large factories and developed strategies centred on the demands advanced by the semiskilled work-force. Collective bargaining became widespread, in so far as it represented not only the most efficient mechanism of distribution but, above all, a system of rules which guaranteed the stability that both workers and employers required (Accornero 1988).

The decline of the Fordist model and the rise of post-Fordist systems of production (Boyer 1988) had many aspects and stemmed from a variety of causes. At the most general level, as we have seen, the search by companies for greater flexibility was a common response, although one that took various forms, to the volatility of markets and to increased competition among firms. This was accompanied by the increased diversification and complexity of the overall production system. One effect of these developments on industrial relations was, initially, the triggering of widespread demands among employers for deregulation – that is, the scrapping of previous rules, established by law or by bargaining, which employers regarded as rigidity factors. Deregulation was sometimes viewed as the absence of rules, and hence as an attempt to replace the unions and collective bargaining with management's direct control of its relationships with workers – that is, a return to 'free' individual bargaining. However (as will become clearer later), this could also have signified, and often did, a desire to create new rules, ones based on the bargaining with the unions of certain forms of flexibility and mobility and on the closer identification of workers with their company.

Having briefly contrasted trends in the 1980s and 1990s with the traditional organization of production, I can now turn to those specific aspects of change which had the most significant impact on industrial relations. The reorganization of production during the 1980s was, in fact, the outcome of very different processes, each of which had its own specific consequences.

The first, and most widely discussed, process of change generated by market volatility and the requirement of greater company competitiveness was the introduction of new technologies, with their concomitant profound transformation of the organization of work. Although this process mainly affected firms exposed to international competition, all the sectors of the economy were to some extent involved. The second process was the diffusion of small firms closely tied to the big ones. This development equally affected sectors in decline and companies which were highly competitive on international markets and equipped with advanced technology. This process has been closely studied in Italy (Brusco 1986; Bagnasco 1988), but there is by now considerable evidence of its importance in other countries as well. The third process involved in the profound reorganization of production was the restructuring of companies and sectors in decline: steel, textiles, shipbuilding and, in some countries, the chemicals industry (Mény and Wright 1987; Pichierri 1989). In this case, reorganization mainly involved layoffs of redundant workers, the closedown and reconversion of plants and attempts at more efficient management. The fourth process to exert a major impact on industrial relations was the expansion (and/or splitting off from the parent company) of business-related services (often called 'the advanced tertiary sector'): marketing, public relations, assistance to customers, tax consultancy, advertising and so on.

As many disparate studies have shown – for example, Piore and Sabel (1984) in the United States, Kern and Schumann (1984) and Streeck (1987) in Germany, Boyer (1986) in France – the onset of these phenomena induced the managements of many firms to rethink the organization of work as well. A number of studies have documented the following: the abandonment of the previous sharp distinction between conception and execution; the increased skills content of many jobs; and the changed nature of control over work and of the functions of hierarchy and rules created to deal with the problem. To sum up – albeit in terms open to doubt and criticism – human intelligence has increasingly been seen as a resource to be used as effectively as possible in the work-place, not as a constraint around which a system of rules is to be erected to discipline it (Kern and Schumann 1984).

The processes of production reorganization just described affected industrial relations in two principal ways. First, by altering the composition of the labour force, they shifted the boundaries of trade-union representation and changed the characteristics and attitudes of those represented. Second, they altered the priorities of firms and therefore the industrial relations strategies of employers.

The principal changes in the composition of the labour force and their effects on industrial relations can be summarized as follows. First, work was 'de-concentrated and de-massified' (Accornero 1988); that is, it became more heterogeneous. The fragmentation of workers' interests and demands consequently increased. The trade unions thus found it more difficult to aggregate demands around hegemonic occupational roles, such as that of the semiskilled worker in the Fordist factory. Yet it was precisely this process which enabled the trade unions to exercise control over collective mobilization and simultaneously maintain their oligopolistic position in centralized political bargaining (Regini 1984).

Second, the emergent sectors of the labour force, now growing in both size and importance, lay outside the trade unions' traditional base. Engineers, employees in the tertiary sector, employees with atypical working arrangements (part-time, seasonal, etc.), workers in small firms, semiartisan workshops or co-operatives providing business-related services: none of these emergent groups were part of the trade unions' traditional sphere of representation. They were, that is, very different from 'typical' workers, with their long tradition of unionization and their customary recourse to collective action in defence of their interests (Chiesi 1990). Consequently, the trade unions encountered increasing difficulties in securing workers' loyalty on the basis of class ideology and collective identity. Instead, a growing number of actual or potential members viewed the unions simply as service agencies which they expected to provide them with services, consultation and protection more efficiently than other organizations. This, of course, was not an altogether new phenomenon: more than a quarter of a century ago, a celebrated study showed the predominance of an instrumental attitude towards trade unions among British workers (Goldthorpe et al. 1968). Overall, however, at least the class unions of continental Europe, more firmly based as they were on solidaristic values and class identity, had until very recently seemed relatively immune to these tendencies.

As far as firms' priorities and the industrial relations strategies of employers were concerned, the common imperative of work flexibility by no means reduced the previous plurality of strategies; it instead led to even more marked diversification, which reflected a contradiction among perceived needs (Streeck 1987). This is not the place for an analytical discussion of various alternatives and discernible trends (see the next chapter on this). Suffice it to point out that in all countries for which adequate research is available, there apparently emerged a plurality of options arranged along a continuum between two extreme strategies.

At one end of the continuum was located a neo-laissez-faire strategy which aimed at deregulation of the employment relationship and at union-free industrial relations, while it restricted the search for work-force consensus to persuasion techniques accompanied by individual bargaining. The most frequently cited cases were those of entire industrial sectors in the United States (e.g., the high-tech sector). Yet attempts by employers to do without trade unions and to replace them with direct personnel management based on individual bargaining with workers were sometimes apparent even in those countries where collective bargaining was still the rule. This was a tendency that naturally alarmed the unions, and perhaps for this reason was a matter of considerable debate. Nevertheless, it soon became clear that, in Europe, its real prospects were rather limited, since the experience of various European companies showed that even in cases where a drastic process of unilaterally managed restructuring had been implemented, once the process was complete it was management itself that raised the problem of re-creating some system of rules agreed to by the unions.

At the other extreme of the continuum stood those companies which had always viewed the joint management with the unions of production reorganization as inevitable. By 'joint management' I mean not just collective bargaining over the consequences of organizational change, but the practice among employers of taking prior consultation, providing information and seeking trade-union consensus on the reorganization processes to implement. One notes with interest that this second strategy was not confined to countries with a tradition of highly consensual industrial relations and of predominantly national-level concertation; it characterized even entire industrial sectors in other countries as well. And although management rarely made this strategy explicit, several studies showed that it was often tacitly adopted in the restructuring of firms. Even in countries like the United Kingdom, which in the 1980s had neo-laissez-faire and antiunion governments – and in which one would have expected employers to seek to eliminate the unions more vigorously and with greater likelihood of success – plant-level industrial relations continued to function with a considerable degree of co-operation (Batstone 1984; Terry 1985; Edwards et al. 1992).

As a result of these very different employers' strategies, some scholars in the 1980s discerned the possibility of an expansion of dualism (Goldthorpe 1984). On the one hand, flexibility and deregulation would be achieved through the growth of the informal economy and of those sectors (e.g., the tertiary sector, especially its 'advanced' branch) in which the unions were practically nonexistent, so that the area dominated by collective bargaining and the traditional institutions of industrial relations would shrink. On the other, firms in which a certain amount of active co-operation by the workforce was still necessary – or even increased in importance as new production methods were introduced – would seek to develop forms of micro-corporatism based on incentives which enhanced employees' identification with the company rather than with the rest of the working class, and on the involvement of local trade unions.

This latter process has been dubbed the 'Japanization' of industrial relations (Streeck 1984), a process envisaged not only as weakening the trade unions' political role, but as dividing workers – even those working in the same firm. One section of the work-force could be managed according to market criteria, while the other would be 'courted' in order to secure its identification with, and therefore loyalty to, the company. As a consequence, trade-union power and industrial relations in general would fragment even further. And perhaps the temptation would increase to create forms of micro-corporatist unionism –

in the traditional sense of priority being given to the security and interests of core workers, to the detriment of more general class interests.

This scenario seemed quite plausible in those countries where the trade-union movement had managed to attain a position of considerable institutional power, in both the factory and the political system. The institutions that reflected this power would not be abolished *tout court*. But employers could aim to erode (helped, of course, by the phenomena discussed earlier) the union movement's capacities of aggregation and to replace them with a more fragmented system of industrial relations, which in turn would correspond to the segmentation of the work-force's market power in companies and sectors.

THE CONSEQUENCES OF DIVERSIFICATION

Changes in the composition of the labour force, and hence in the characteristics of those represented by the unions, were just as profound in the 1980s as those that took place in the organization of production. To a certain extent, these changes stemmed from the reorganization processes that I discussed in the preceding section. But in large measure they also depended on more general sociocultural processes, ones not directly tied to the productive system.

The changes in the labour force were both structural (i.e., relative to its composition) and subjective (i.e., relative to attitudes). Three main processes were involved. The first of them has already been mentioned, in so far as it derived from the changes discussed in the preceding section; it therefore requires no further analysis. Suffice it to point out that the structure of the labour force changed because, as a consequence of the reorganization of production, occupational roles became more diversified: those with no tradition of unionization increased in number, while even among industrial workers there was a greater heterogeneity of demands.

The second process was the growth in the number and influence of workers with uncertain status in the labour market. The examples are numerous, ranging from wage-earners who were also self-employed, sometimes preparing to become small entrepreneurs, to early retirees working in the informal economy, to free lances with a de facto stable work relationship with an employer. What all these 'atypical' categories had in common was their uncertain status in the labour market. Either they combined some sort of casual work with social security benefits or they stood midway between self-employed workers and wage-earners. Thus, in certain respects they resembled 'normal' wage-earners, while in others they were very different from them.

The third process was a general increase in the flexibility in work performance rules and working time (Accornero 1988) which did not necessarily meet the demand for flexibility advanced by firms. For example, many highly skilled workers viewed their work as incorporating greater versatility, mobility, initiative and autonomy than was normally envisaged by company job descriptions or by the regulations negotiated by the trade unions in order to constrain managerial discretionary powers. Flexibility was offered in this case by workers with strong bargaining power in order to imbue their job with features more typical of the professions or self-employment. Often, it was the firms which opposed this tendency, thus displaying in practice that rigidity which in theory was their avowed enemy.

As a further example, many categories of workers (especially young people and women) were more than willing to accept various forms of flexitime, short work cycles, alternating periods of work and nonwork and so on (Chiesi 1990). In this case, too, their needs could conflict with management's conception of flexibility, and even more so with the unions' traditional view of what the real interests of workers were and how they should be protected.

These changes had various effects on industrial relations, effects which only partly overlapped with those produced by the reorganization of production. First, there were the two consequences that I pointed out earlier: the unions found it increasingly difficult to aggregate demands and to identify general class interests, and a growing number of workers viewed the trade union as just another service-providing agency; that is, their relationship with it became purely instrumental, no longer based on ideological identity.

Second, as their identification with the working class as a whole and with its ambitions for the economic and political transformation of capitalist society grew increasingly tenuous, many workers developed a closer identification with the firm or the production unit in which they worked. Although this was not an entirely new phenomenon, its size and forms were nonetheless relatively novel. For instance, the success of Japanese-style quality circles, not only in the United States but in many Western European countries, would have been unthinkable ten years earlier. Accordingly, this was less a revival of old forms of micro-corporatism among relatively privileged groups of workers than greater identification with the company as a source of identity and values.

Finally, a number of studies noted a certain increase in individual bargaining between employers and workers – even ones without highly marketable skills or crucial roles in the productive process. Of course, this development stemmed chiefly from the already-mentioned concern of many employers to individualize work relations. There is no doubt, however, that it also signalled the willingness of numerous workers to accept this option, often in polemical reaction to a type of union-managed collective bargaining which they regarded as too inflexible. In other words, the traditional endeavour of a trade union to impose uniform standards on employers was now seen by many employees as an unwarranted simplification of their needs and abilities.

There were, therefore, multiple factors which induced both employers and workers to seek greater flexibility in the employment relationship. Flexibility was accordingly an objective shared by both of them to some extent, although they often differed radically over the best means to achieve it.

For employers, in fact, labour flexibility meant the relatively unconstrained use of their work-forces – which did not necessarily imply the absence of rules, but acceptance of only those rules (legislative or contractual) that were not too rigid, uniform or standardized. Since the firms' objective was evidently to increase productivity and to achieve full utilization of all production inputs, their search for flexibility tended to be in areas which most readily lent themselves to it: changing the rules on labour market entry and exit, on internal mobility and on pay systems and conditions of employment.

For workers, too, flexibility meant that they viewed their work and working time as less standardized, uniform and rigid. But the objective in their case was to enhance their skills, versatility and on-the-job autonomy, and also to base the relationship between work and leisure on their life-projects and life-styles, rather than on the needs of production.

Hence, flexibility seemed to be in the interests of both workers and employers. Yet at the same time it provided a further arena for antagonism between them (Hyman 1991; Regini 1992). As labour flexibility gradually acquires central importance for both employers and workers, it may change the scope and rules of industrial relations; these will be based less on an exchange of goods – as in traditional bargaining – and more on an attempt at joint regulation of the employment relationship. Joint regulation need not necessarily signify co-determination; and yet it is certainly very different from antagonistic relationships or even reciprocal noninterference. What it does mean is that methods for organizing work performance can become an arena of simultaneous convergence and conflict: convergence on the principle of flexibility, conflict over the forms it should take.

7

The problem of consensus in production

The intense debate of the 1980s on employers' strategies for the reorganization of production and work (Piore and Sabel 1984; Kern and Scumann 1984; Boyer 1986; Dore 1986; Streeck 1987) probably paid insufficient attention to the variability of managerial attitudes towards the use of human resources and the problem of in-company consensus. Not that these issues were omitted from analysis; indeed, they received considerable attention in both the social sciences and management literature.[1] But they were too frequently taken simply as corollaries to more general changes in production patterns – as phenomena, therefore, that did not require specific explanation. In other words, the variability in managerial policies of labour regulation – a concept that I clarify later – was for the most part interpreted in a straightforward manner as an aspect and a consequence of the diversification of production models.

The premise of this chapter is instead that the different strategies pursued by European employers in personnel management and industrial relations depend only in part on productive, technological and organizational choices. Institutional and social factors play no less important a role, during a phase in which previous action models have proved clearly inadequate and in which uncertainty has consequently increased. My intention here is, first, to provide an analytical scheme which helps us to understand the range and significance of the search for greater labour consensus that has characterized the strategies of various European companies in recent years. I shall then use this analytical scheme to explain the more general changes that have taken place in the 1980s and 1990s. Finally, I shall examine a number of differences among the European countries and the factors that explain these differences.

MANAGERIAL POLICIES FOR LABOUR REGULATION AND THE SEARCH FOR CONSENSUS: AN ANALYTICAL FRAMEWORK

By 'managerial policies for labour regulation'[2] I mean the rules and practices followed by the management of a particular firm in structuring both employment relationships and the use of the work-force and its interaction with workers and their collective representatives. When referring to methods of regulating the employment relationship and the use of the work-force, it is customary to use the terms 'personnel policies' (or 'human resource management and development') and 'work organization'. The rules and practices adopted in structuring interaction with workers and their trade-union representatives are usually included in the category 'industrial relations'. But for reasons that I hope will become clear, I prefer to consider these two kinds of managerial policy jointly.

Numerous aspects of the employment relationship and the use of the work-force are structured according to different rules and practices. By way of example, and without my attempting to draw up an exhaustive list, these aspects range from work-force entry and exit from the firm, to pay and incentive schemes (including company welfare programmes), to job assignment and internal mobility, to the organization of working time, to skill formation with its associated training and career development programmes. In order to regulate each of these aspects or elements of the employment relationship, a company management may, of course, decide to rely exclusively on its own organizational and hierarchical power. But in addressing the general problem of ensuring the continuity of production, and especially the ever more pressing problem of guaranteeing product quality and organizational flexibility, most managements seek to secure at least minimal work-force consensus on the rules and practices to adopt.

However, even when a management considers the consensus of its work-force to be of major importance, it has various options available with which to attain it. The management's principal choice is between, on the one hand, seeking direct consensus by offering substantive benefits to workers – that is, solutions which bring advantages or bonuses to those who co-operate – and, on the other, aiming to involve their representatives in regulation so that consensus can be obtained indirectly.

What I have called 'interaction with workers and their collective representatives' also has several aspects: the intensity of negotiation and other relationships, such as meetings for information or consultation, the amount and kind of resources provided for workers' representatives, reactions to conflictual behaviour and so on. Of course, these aspects of interaction, too, can be regulated in different ways, that is, structured according to different rules and practices. And in this case as well, a management which seeks to predicate its interaction with workers and their representatives on consensus has various options.

A management may try, first of all, to enhance the workers' symbolic identification with the firm (by means of 'sensitization campaigns' centred on production targets and problems) or to encourage their more active involvement in company performance. The management may restrict itself to offering recognition and resources to workers' representatives in exchange for their noninterference in managerial prerogatives, or it may foster their participation in productive, technological and organizational decisions by resorting to various forms of consultation, joint committees or similar procedures.

Hence, managerial policies for labour regulation differ not only in terms of the extent or intensity of consensus being sought (which is the rather obvious dimension on which traditional typologies are constructed); they also differ in terms of the type of consensus that these policies aim to achieve. The alternatives, therefore, are not just between passive acceptance and active participation, but also between consensus as the outcome of direct relationships with workers and consensus mediated by relationships with their representatives, and between general consensus with the firm and consensus solely over specific decisions relative to the employment relationship.

Labour consensus is a multidimensional variable, and it therefore cannot be reduced to the overly simple alternatives with which a number of personnel management and industrial relations experts are accustomed to work. If account is not taken of this plurality of the dimensions to the search for consensus, it is impossible to grasp the real alternatives of labour regulation available to European firms in the 1990s.

Figure 3 presents a typology which incorporates these various dimensions. This typology is not a descriptive classification of the entire range of managerial policies implemented in practice. Nor does it include other important dimensions (e.g., the degree of homogeneity in regulation, i.e., whether it concerns only certain groups of workers or the entire company work-force). It is merely an analytical tool intended to bring out both the differences in managerial behaviour among firms and changes over time (as the discussion in the next section will show).

1. The variable 'types of managerial policies' takes account of the fact that either firms may seek to establish individual relationships with workers and to regulate the employment relationship directly, or they may rely on the mediation of the workers' representatives. In both cases, the management's intention may simply be to obtain passive endorsement of its objectives and methods, or else to foster more active participation. (This is the dimension that comes closest to what I call the 'intensity or extent' of the consensus sought.)

What ultimately counts for management is some degree of employee cooperation in the functioning of the productive process. However, the unions and the workers' representatives may, depending on the context, either be valuable instruments with which to achieve such co-operation or the means whereby it is obstructed. Management can exert only limited control over

TYPES OF MANAGERIAL POLICIES

SCOPE OF CONSENSUS	Direct labour regulation		Regulation through representatives	
	I. Unilateral management	II. Workers' involvement	III. Negotiated management	IV. Representatives' involvement
General consensus with the firm	*Persuasion* (consensus as compliance)	*Direct active participation* (consensus as shared goals)	*Recognition of rights and power* (consensus as exchange)	*Procedural strategic participation* (consensus as joint management)
Consensus on specific aspects of employment relation	*Substantive involvement* (consensus as compensation)		*Regulatory involvement* (consensus as pragmatic ad hoc co-operation)	

Figure 3. Dimensions of the search for consensus by management.

which of these alternatives prevails, since they depend to a large extent on previous traditions and on more general trade-union strategies. However, it is not difficult to predict that management will behave accordingly, either by favouring interaction with the collective representatives or by seeking to establish direct relationships with employees when this does not entail prohibitive costs.

Whichever option is taken, the intensity of the co-operation sought is, as I have said, extremely variable. In situations where management places high trust in its workers or their representatives, it will probably solicit active participation as a contribution to company performance. In situations of low trust, the concern to avoid interference with managerial prerogatives will prevail, reducing the search for collaboration to that for simple compliance with managerial decisions – compliance that firms can either seek to impose ideologically on their employees or to exchange with benefits accruing to the employees' representatives.

The four types of managerial policies for labour regulation which derive from joint consideration of these two dimensions correspond in part to those most commonly found in the industrial relations literature. Of course, this literature often uses terms other than unilateral management, workers' involvement, negotiated management and representatives' involvement. And intermediate or partially different types may be proposed, especially when the intention is to stress the role of conflict and power relationships more than the forms taken by the search for consensus. But apart from differences in terminology and the number of types identified, many current typologies are basically the same as that set out in the first row of Figure 3 (i.e., the types indicated by numerals I to IV).

2. A variable largely neglected by the literature is what I have labelled here the 'scope' of the search for consensus, a scope that may vary irrespective of the intensity of the co-operation that management wishes to obtain from the workers or their representatives. The typologies used in the literature – and also the four types I have just discussed – implicitly assume that management is interested, to a greater or lesser extent, in some degree of general consensus among workers with the firm, that is, their willingness in principle to co-operate in the achievement of targets and in the running of the firm itself. But it is extremely important, for reasons given later, to bear in mind that management may be less interested in this general kind of consensus than in securing some degree of co-operation in structuring specific but crucial aspects of the employment relationship – that is, in securing consent to individual regulative decisions, whatever the general climate of co-operation within the firm may be.

The interest of managements in 'general consensus' varies widely according to their traditions, cultures and managerial styles. This has traditionally led firms to differentiate themselves by adopting distinct and sometimes opposing models. Different conceptions of the degree of worker consensus on the objectives of the firm deemed necessary by those responsible for running it, and of ways in which this consensus can be secured either directly or by union action made compatible with production needs, have generated a variety of solutions.

I use the term 'persuasion' to refer to attempts to obtain workers' compliance which rely on techniques of symbolic-ideological involvement. These may be traditional techniques (paternalistic practices, the condoning of irregular behaviour) or newer ones (direct communication policies). But in all cases they are intended, though with greater or lesser success, to foster the individual worker's identification with his or her firm.

On the other hand, a management may seek the 'direct active participation' of workers in the firm's goals by soliciting their active contribution to company performance and by encouraging their responsible involvement in its results, using instruments such as quality circles. Although of variable effectiveness, these techniques are not designed solely to secure the workers' compliance with management directives; they are also intended to have them share the constraints on the firm and actively contribute to the achievement of its objectives.

'Recognition' of trade unions and/or works councils as the legitimate representatives of the workers, and as partners in the negotiated regulation of labour, is the solution traditionally adopted by managements seeking to preserve their discretionary powers, but at the same time amenable to collective bargaining on the consequences of their decisions and on the share of benefits to be distributed to labour. In this case, workers' co-operation is sought through the mediation of their representatives, to which management offers not involvement in management of the firm, but power and resources (material or symbolic: rights, information, etc.) in exchange for behaviour in compliance with negotiated rules.

The collective representatives, on the other hand, may be involved in at least some strategic decisions relative to the firm's productive, technological, organizational or market decisions. They may be consulted systematically over these decisions, or they may participate in the management of the firm through formal procedures or such institutions as co-determination or similar methods – whence derives the term 'procedural strategic participation' used here for this model of consensus search.

Unlike the classic problem of general consensus with the firm (i.e., with its aim and management), the question of 'specific consensus' over individual choices in the regulation of the employment relationship is not invariably of the same importance for firms. It presumably becomes particularly urgent when they find themselves passing through a period of rapid and profound change in the organization of work. If certain aspects of the employment relationship (e.g., working hours, internal mobility) require rapid reorganization – that is, if they must be subjected to rules markedly different from previous ones – management will probably seek the approval of the workers affected by these new measures, approval that may be largely independent of their endorsement of the firm's overall objectives.

Of course, as in the case of the traditional problem of general consensus, some employers may simply deny that the problem exists and rely instead on hierarchical authority, blackmail and all the other opportunities provided by the basic asymmetry of power between employer and employees, in order to achieve their objectives. However, to an even greater extent than in the classic situation, it is extremely difficult to attain a satisfactory solution by means of the simple exercise of such power. If, in fact, the change is to be sufficiently rapid and effective, it must not encounter strong resistance. And in many firms its success is largely inconceivable without a minimum of co-operation or approval by the workers affected by the new rules.

Regardless of their traditional style of personnel and industrial relations management, therefore, numerous employers would in this case be induced to search pragmatically for their workers' co-operation over the aspects of the employment relationship requiring re-regulation. What they need is involvement which is restricted to these specific aspects – something less than endorsement of the overall objectives of the firm, but something more than merely passive compliance with the new rules: a commitment to the solution of problems as and when they arise, a willingness to provide the necessary feedback on decisions made by management – in short, co-operation to ensure that change produces the expected outcomes.

In all the situations in which this kind of specific consensus becomes of major importance for employers, the traditional antithesis between managerial strategies based on low trust in workers and those based on high trust in them becomes blurred. What is at stake in these cases, in fact, is 'limited trust'. This, however, is not simply a situation located midway along an ideal continuum; rather, it is the outcome of a pragmatic adaptation process which can coexist with different general styles of labour regulation. The latter simply become less able to influence concrete behaviours – that is, less relevant to a wide range of practical results.

Thus, certain employers may be prompted to seek the active co-operation of workers or trade unions over certain aspects of the employment relationship while they persist with a general policy of noninterference by the latter in their decisions, a policy which consequently loses some of its practical significance. On the other hand, employers traditionally more sensitive to trade-union pressures for industrial democracy may preserve information and consultation procedures but reduce them to an essentially symbolic role, while simultaneously developing new techniques to secure individual workers' consensus over a different use of the work-force.

So when the scope and objectives of interaction are restricted to the consensual regulation of certain specific aspects of the employment relationship alone, what I earlier called the 'intensity' or the 'extent' of the work-force's involvement is more the unexpected outcome of a series of pragmatic decisions regarding which components of the employment contract should be changed, and in what way, than a consistent policy of industrial relations and personnel management. Paradoxically, one can find firms which are traditionally favourable towards trade unions' participation but in which the actual extent of union involvement in specific aspects of the employment relationship is still limited, while others are in principle opposed to any interference with managerial prerogatives but find themselves forced to involve their employees or their representative in a series of ad hoc regulative decisions which are not part of any participative design. For these reasons, therefore, when the scope and objectives of the interaction are specific and limited, the sharp distinctions between types I and II and between types III and IV in the typology presented earlier lose their significance (and therefore do not appear in the bottom row of Figure 3).

We may nevertheless assume that a management accustomed to bargaining directly and individually with its employees will seek to obtain this kind of specific and limited consensus by offering substantive benefits proportional to the potential contribution of their co-operation to the successful outcome of change. In firms in which there instead exists a tradition of industrial relations, managements will more likely offer the workers' representatives some sort of involvement in the re-regulation of the employment relationship – that is, information, consultation or negotiation on those aspects which need to be changed. The former type of search for consensus takes the form of direct compensation for the willingness to co-operate: hence, I use the term 'substantive involvement' for it. The latter form I call 'regulatory involvement', because in this case the search for consensus is a bid for pragmatic and ad hoc co-operation in the regulation of labour.

APPLYING THE ANALYTICAL FRAMEWORK TO EUROPEAN COMPANIES

A number of recent studies conducted in Europe furnish valuable data and observations on changes over time and, especially, on differences among firms regarding managerial strategies of labour regulation.[3] The accuracy with which the analytical scheme set out in the preceding section interprets these changes and differences can therefore be put to the test.

In the 1970s, the predominant image of company industrial relations in Europe – especially in Britain, France and Italy – was one of a system of interaction marked by a low level of trust. Almost everywhere, the unions enjoyed considerable power and support in the work-place, but their culture remained predominantly adversarial. Employers, for their part, conceded considerable recognition and resources to the unions, sometimes because they were forced to reluctantly acknowledge existing power relationships, sometimes because they hoped for social peace and co-operation in exchange.

Although this was the image that predominated among labour analysts, however, it was already clear that it only partially corresponded to reality. A more accurate picture would have shown the coexistence of different kinds of interaction. Some form of negotiated management (i.e., the third type of managerial policy in the typology of Figure 3) became the rule in many – probably most – European large industrial firms, in which recognition of the rights and power of trade unions seemed almost unavoidable if the minimum of consensus necessary for the management and pursuit of company objectives was to be achieved. However, in small firms – and also in some of the large ones, especially in countries and regions with weak unionism – unilateral methods of work-force management were common, and the search for consensus relied mainly on persuasion techniques based on the ideology of a community of interests. Workers' involvement practices – that is, the encouragement of direct and active participation by the work-force – were instead employed in the more dynamic industrial districts, especially those located in the culturally and politically homogeneous areas of the Third Italy. Finally, in countries like Germany, as well as in certain industrial holdings in other countries (e.g., IRI in Italy) and multinational companies, legislation on co-determination, contractual agreements or independently established practice involved workers' representatives in firms' strategies.

Of course, there were also a number of mixed cases. But I would maintain that this image of the substantial coexistence, throughout the 1970s, of distinct and opposing models of managerial policies of labour regulation is generally accurate. I deliberately use the term 'model' to stress that the choice of a particular alternative was often a value-laden one, not simply the outcome of pragmatic decisions, and above all because once a model had been chosen, it constituted the scheme of reference for action and structured a whole set of managerial behaviours.

The early 1980s were a turning-point. Whereas at the national level industrial relations were either adversarial or stagnant, the situation began to change rapidly at the company level. On the one hand, the more innovative and dynamic small firms – in which policies geared to workers' involvement predominated – proved better equipped than large ones to cope with the increasing volatility of markets and the greater severity of international competition. On the other, many large firms facing difficulties began a long process of restructuring and adjustment which entailed not only a high rate of technological innovation but also major work reorganization to increase flexibility. Since these processes have already been analysed in previous chapters, this brief mention of them should suffice here. What I wish to stress, though, is this: not only can these processes be fitted into the analytical scheme presented in the preceding section, but the scheme can be used to provide a richer interpretation of them.

In fact, when the studies cited are re-examined in this light, one finds that, for the majority of firms in the 1980s, the crucial problem of labour regulation was no longer the achievement of general consensus on the overall aims of the firm, but concrete co-operation in the reorganization of specific aspects of the employment relationship (in general, those relating to the more flexible use of the work-force). For this reason, the scope and objectives of managerial interaction with workers and unions changed. Whatever broad-gauge model of industrial relations they adopted, many employers found themselves forced to seek pragmatically some co-operation over the aspects of work that required re-regulation. But this was only part of the story, the part which has already been anticipated in the preceding section.

The story has a second part, which centres on the alternative between 'substantive' and 'regulatory' forms of involvement presented in the typology of Figure 3 as two theoretically distinct options. During the 1980s, this sharp antithesis became blurred, as many firms experimented with both kinds of involvement: the first offered directly to workers involved in organizational change, the second to their representatives. We may define these phenomena as manifestations of a pragmatic eclecticism on the part of management and view them as stemming from two main factors.

The first and rather obvious factor lay in managerial objectives themselves, which in those years were the re-regulation of individual aspects of the employment relationship. Now it is possible, of course, that on one or more of these aspects (e.g., internal mobility) a company management might seek to establish direct relationships with individual workers, whereas on others (e.g., the organization of working hours) it might decide to involve the unions. In the examples cited, the management might behave like this because the unions endorsed the objective of more flexible working time but opposed internal mobility, or for various other reasons.[4] In other words, given the multiple dimensions of the employment relationship, the most practical way (for management) to implement change in one of them might prove much less effective in another. In periods of rapid change, particularly when crucial problems of work organization are confronted as and when they arise, a management is more concerned to find satisfactory, albeit incoherent, solutions to these problems than to reaffirm the general principles that mould its style of handling personnel and industrial relations.

The second and more important factor in the diffusion of pragmatic eclecticism was the growth of conflicting pressures on employers – pressures more complex and more divergent than before, and such as to render clear-cut choices more difficult. On the one hand, various factors were working against the unions – that is, against employers' interest in involving them in the re-regulation of work. The overall weakness of the unions, in terms of both their capacity for representation and their organizational resources, offered employers a tempting opportunity to take revenge for what they saw as the excessive use of power by the unions in the preceding decade, by marginalizing them. The fall-off in the political and institutional support previously enjoyed by the unions reinforced the process. Moreover, intensified competition on international markets increased employers' impatience with rules and practices now considered to be excessively constraining or rigid.

On the other hand, management found itself exposed to pressures working in the opposite direction which induced it not to exclude the unions, but to involve them more closely in labour regulation. First and foremost, the moderation shown in most cases by the unions – or better, their substantial compliance with and internalization of the corporate imperative of flexibility – meant that their behaviour often encouraged change rather than hindered it. Since work-force resistance to innovation can be more easily overcome if unions are allies rather than adversaries, this, in many cases, was an opportunity that was swiftly taken up. Moreover, the need to forge an alliance with the unions – against competing firms, against public institutions in order to obtain financial and political support and also against the groups of workers bound to be the losers in the restructuring process – was strongly felt by employers, who saw themselves as particularly vulnerable now that they had started along the difficult road of adjustment and were therefore in need of social legitimation.

The combined effect of a shift of interaction towards specific aspects of the re-regulation of the employment relationship, and the spread of managerial practices distinguished by pragmatic eclecticism, was twofold. First, managerial policies for labour regulation became more diversified in the 1980s than they had been in the preceding decade. Even similar enterprises belonging to the same sector often adopted different approaches to certain aspects of the employment relationship, and identical ones to others. Second, the average level of co-operation in European industrial relations increased considerably, even though this was still largely pragmatic and secluded co-operation. The scenario I have depicted so far, therefore, highlights a dual process at work in Europe during the 1980s, one which we may call 'convergence in the diversification' of solutions to labour regulation problems adopted by firms and a 'rise in the average rate of co-operation' in the industrial system.

NATIONAL DIFFERENCES AND THEIR ORIGINS

It is difficult to measure the extent and intensity of the involvement of workers' representatives in managerial decisions. The number of formal and informal meetings is not a reliable indicator; even less reliable is the fact that in one company fewer aspects of the work relationship (such as compensation, training, overtime and shiftwork) are subject to consensual decisions than in another, since this may depend on a number of factors. Actors' perceptions of either the social climate of the company or the degree of their reciprocal influence may also be misleading. The nature of their relationship is at times perceived as consultation, at others as information and at others still as negotiation. The difficulty becomes even greater when one compares different countries with different industrial relations cultures.

In spite of these difficulties, however, research consistently shows that union involvement in the regulation of work is more extensive, constant and effective in some European countries than in others. For instance, it is well known that in Germany workers' representatives are far more closely involved in various aspects of labour regulation than they are in France or Spain. Even so, recent research has brought to light certain aspects that could not have been anticipated.

One unexpected finding is the fact that the legal rights of information, consultation or negotiation are apparently of minor importance. I shall return to this observation later in order to suggest the potentially contradictory effects of these rights on the extension of co-operative relations. For the time being, suffice it to observe that in the three countries just mentioned such rights (though of different natures and to various degrees) are more extensively and formally declared, while in Britain and Italy the law plays a minor role in this area. Yet companies in the latter countries bear a distinctly closer resemblance to German companies, in terms of co-operative relations and union involvement in the regulation of work, than they do to Spanish, and especially French, ones.

A similar observation applies to the degree of formality in labour–management meetings and relations in general, a feature which depends partly on how industrial relations are regulated by the law and partly on the more general culture of the actors concerned. Most agreements, meetings and so on usually follow fixed rules, schedules and procedures in both German and Spanish companies, whereas in Italy and Britain a large proportion of decentralized relations are administered in highly informal ways. Again, this does not seem to have clear consequences on the extent and stability of union participation in the regulation of work.

A further observation is that the intensity of co-operation is not necessarily correlated with each actor's willingness to adapt to the views of the other. To take the example of labour flexibility, in some German companies – where labour–management co-operation is in a certain sense built into the system and therefore very high – negotiation over working time has continued for years with neither party trying too hard to force agreement on the other. By contrast, in British companies, where co-operation is more limited and depends on calculations which may change rapidly, and where an economistic tradition prevails, the unions are often ready to 'sell' labour flexibility or, better, to forgo their veto powers in exchange for wage increases.

Finally, it would be wrong to assume that the differences in the actual degree of union participation in the regulation of work reflect only the policies of company management. These differences are often the outcome of differing orientations among the trade unions as well. This is clearly the case of the Spanish and French unions, which sometimes treat greater involvement in the company with suspicion, preferring to negotiate from clearly distinct positions and to rely on the law (especially in the Spanish case) to give more general support to their negotiating stance. But the trade unions of other countries, too, may display different orientations. For instance, in both British and German companies, the worker representatives sometimes express their dissatisfaction with the 'excess' of information provided them by the company management because they do not know how to handle it. Far from demanding greater involvement in company decisions, worker representatives tend in these cases to interpret management behaviour as an attempt to overwhelm them with information, thereby preventing them from doing their work efficiently.

As we have seen, the search for consensus in the 1980s and 1990s has not pursued only the traditional route of involving workers' representatives in decisions concerning production issues. Attempts by company management to establish direct relationships with individual workers have increased as well.

These attempts take a variety of forms. British and Spanish firms tend to inform workers directly about company objectives by means of team briefings and the like. Managers in French companies have long preferred quality circles as a means to involve employees more directly in issues related to production problems and product quality. In Germany, where the focus on quality is part of the traditional job consciousness of (especially skilled) labour, where abundant information is usually provided through the institutions of co-determination and where wage increases cannot officially be negotiated at the plant level, the emphasis has been more on selective monetary incentives, such as participation in profit schemes, employee shareholding and various forms of noncontractual earnings. In Italian companies, all these various kinds of individualized relationship have become fairly common.

Whatever concrete form they may take, these attempts to establish direct relations with individual workers have not, by and large, been suggested as alternatives to relations mediated by the unions and workers' representatives; quite the contrary. In several case studies of companies, the managers interviewed stressed the noninterference of these methods with the unions and their role in industrial relations. When one thinks of how a comparable group of North American managers would probably have answered, the similarity among the European managers' views appears quite striking.

However, the views expressed by the workers' representatives did not always coincide with the management's. Whereas in the German, Italian and British companies, unionists were generally ready to confirm the management's interpretation, in that they did not feel bypassed by these attempts, their French and Spanish counterparts were more reluctant to do so.

One notes, however, especially in the latter countries, that these efforts by management have apparently been directed mainly at those groups in the work-force (white-collar workers, foremen, technicians) which are less unionized. Hence, both interpretations are in a sense correct. Since the principal aim of these policies is to win the confidence and support of employees who are not part of the traditional union base, they may be seen both as not interfering with the normal processes of industrial relations and as an attempt to limit the range of union influence. After all, an alternative method of securing consensus, if successful, is always proof that the collective representation and intermediation of interests is but one of the possible alternatives available to managers and workers. Only when managers are convinced that unions are not merely a second-best option which they can use *faute de mieux* to govern the labour process, and only when they believe instead that the unions may constitute an important resource, will they resist the temptation to circumvent their functions and power.

Institutional factors are of major importance in explaining the differences in the industrial relations strategies just described. I shall briefly comment on two of them: the role of legal rights to information, consultation and negotiation in different national contexts, and the type of worker representatives present in the companies studied.

1. I have already pointed out that extensive legislation on the rights of workers' representatives to be informed, consulted and so forth on a series of issues does not per se determine a high degree of actual union participation in management decisions. Although the existence of co-determination laws in Germany might lead one to such a conclusion, the degree of union involvement is higher in Italian and British firms than in Spanish and French ones, despite the greater role of union-supportive legislation in the latter.

Closer inspection, however, reveals two major, though contradictory, effects of union rights legislation on the interaction between management and unions. First, rights to information, consultation or participation in joint committees on a number of issues increase the technical content of the task of workers' representatives and may therefore induce them to co-operate with management, or to oppose it, on specific aspects and details rather than rely on generic slogans. This, however, seems to be only the case of German firms, where the *Betriebsräte* are strong and management is obliged to take cognizance of their points of view. By contrast, French and Spanish unions are too weak to influence the way that work is regulated. Hence, they conceive of their task in less technical terms, and they may even resent being overwhelmed by information which they cannot control.

Second, although legislation on information and consultation rights augments the functions of the workers' representatives on a number of issues – such as, typically, overtime or work shifts – it also has the effect of freezing the boundaries between unilateral and consensual regulation. In fact, if companies abide by the law, the workers' representatives have less incentive to question which issues should be subject to consensual regulation, while the management feels that a sufficient amount of participation has been offered to the unions and that it is not obliged to expand their involvement. In other words, the issue of the extent and intensity of information, consultation and negotiation is effectively removed from the industrial relations agenda and no longer performs the function of symbolically measuring the degree of co-operation in management–union relationships. Paradoxically, then, the area of de facto participation may be broader in countries like Italy with few legally defined rights than it is in countries like France and Spain with more extensive legal regulation of management–union interaction.

2. Obviously, when unions are organizationally strong and nonmilitant, employers are more reluctant to fight them and more willing to involve them in decisions than they are when unions are weak and/or conflictual. However, even among companies with strong and nonmilitant unions, behaviour towards them differs rather significantly.

This feature seems to depend on the attitudes that unions have developed towards company needs, attitudes which are pragmatic in some cases and more ideological – in that they stress a clear distinction of functions – in others. In the former case, employers find it advantageous to use unions as a resource in the management of labour, and they establish intense, though often informal, relationships with them. In the latter case, employers tend not to exceed the degree of involvement imposed on them by law or tradition. Managers' values and ideas do not matter greatly in this respect. Even the former type of behaviour, in fact, stems from an opportunistic recognition of the unions' potentially positive role in the re-regulation of labour, and not from greater ideological sympathy with them.

This explains why the boundaries of pragmatic, co-operative behaviour within which employers may consider trade unions to be a resource are, generally speaking, rather narrow. If co-operation is to be valued by employers, it must produce a form of micro-corporatism (i.e., within the corporation borders) even at the expense of weakening the ties between workers' representatives in the work-place and external trade unions. The unions must focus on advancing the interests of the core labour force by accepting a de facto segmentation which hinders their ability to represent both higher (technicians and administrative staff) and marginal (e.g., seasonal) groups of workers. They are confronted by a systematic division between everyday decisions concerning the organization of work in which they are invited to participate and strategic decisions from which they are excluded. More generally, employers are ready to pay an economic cost for the slower and slightly modified decision-making process which results from union participation, but they are reluctant to consider the possibility of substantially modifying their decisions.

The managerial search for workers' consensus and the discovery of the unions' potentially positive role in production do not, in other words, imply a sudden willingness to share authority. To the extent that social peace and flexibility in production are, for European companies, collective goods which, in the current phase of industrial organization, can be better achieved through unions and industrial relations institutions than against them, employers are likely to continue to expand union participation. But the scope, stability and significance of such participation will remain open issues until it is based on self-interested calculations and voluntary behaviour on management's side, rather than on renewed union power and its translation into institutional advantages.

8

An emblematic case: industrial adjustment
and micro-concertation in Italy

The changes in the organization of firms that took place during the 1980s in Italy[1] (in line with the more general trends described in Chapter 6) were exceptionally far-reaching and rapid. No one could have predicted their range and impact as the decade began. In the late 1970s, in fact, large firms and unions seemed to be locked in disastrous stalemate. Although the unions were greatly weakened, they still retained sufficient power to block, if they wished, successful adjustment to an economic environment that had become increasingly uncertain. The firms, for their part, had it in their power to decentralize production to small units operating beyond the control of factory councils, to make selective use of the Wages Guarantee Fund in order to disrupt trade-union organization in the work-place and to introduce new technologies a little at a time, thereby gradually eroding the unions' ability to exercise effective control over labour.

In this situation the only winners were apparently small firms, which were able to take considerable advantage of the wave of decentralization. The so-called Third Italy (central and northeastern), with its economy based on industrial districts – that is, integrated systems of highly flexible small firms (Brusco 1986; Bagnasco 1988) – seemed to encapsulate everything new that Italian industry had to offer and consequently attracted much attention from observers, with the concomitant neglect of both the North-West Italy of earlier industrialization and the Mezzogiorno.

During the 1980s, however, the situation changed extremely rapidly (Barca and Magnani 1989). Beset by several financial difficulties, many large companies managed to break the stalemate by undertaking radical restructuring, which was conducted in most cases, as we shall see, with the active co-operation of the trade unions and only infrequently after overcoming their resistance. Meanwhile, the small firms also transformed themselves, becoming equipped – by means of consortia, various forms of association and in some cases real services provided by local agencies – with institutions and instruments that enabled them to more vigorously resist increasing international competition. This chapter examines the forms that this twofold process of restructuring (by large and by small firms) took and the factors that made it possible.

FIRMS AND RESTRUCTURING

For large firms, generally speaking, the adjustment process meant searching for ever-greater flexibility – that is, the ability to adjust rapidly to increasingly volatile markets. In some cases, firms believed that they could regain competitiveness simply by reducing their labour costs, and they therefore confined themselves to cutting their work-force by resorting to the Wages Guarantee Fund, early retirement plans and the decentralization of production to small units. This strategy, however, largely failed to provide the flexibility required, and many large firms were consequently forced to undertake a profound revision of their organizational criteria, in particular of that guiding principle of mass production: the separation between conception and execution.

I could elaborate the stylized picture set out in Chapter 6 by citing numerous examples of successful adjustment by large Italian firms. For the sake of brevity, however, I shall restrict myself to one emblematic example, that of Montedison at Ferrara (Bordogna 1989). Here the previous petrochemicals complex divided itself into four single-product independent companies – plus a fifth one, Montedipe, which provided services to the others on a quasi-market basis. These services ranged from the technical (the maintenance of equipment, the design of new plant, the testing of feed stocks and final products) to the administrative (bookkeeping, collective bargaining with the unions, management of layoffs, etc.). Top managers were trained to co-ordinate the objectives of the operational units with those of the corporation. So flexible did production become that more than fifty 'changes of campaign' (the firm's term for shifts in production set-up) per year were possible. Many products were developed in direct consultation with the customer. The overall system resembled one of the industrial districts that I shall shortly describe, with the difference that in this case it was the service company, not the local government or employers' associations, which supplied the production units with everything they were unable to obtain themselves.

Similar patterns were revealed by studies of Falck (Regalia 1989), Italtel (Negrelli 1989), Fiat (Locke and Negrelli 1989) and Olivetti (Berta and Michelsons 1989). This is not to imply that these tendencies were unique to Italian large companies, since similar ones have been amply documented elsewhere, for example in Germany (Sabel 1988; Thelen 1991). What is nevertheless specific to them is their extremely rapid occurrence in firms which, in the early 1980s, were still apparently in total paralysis and in a country where only a few years previously it had been practically axiomatic to talk of 'structural' economic and industrial crisis.

Let us now look at the changes that took place in those small firms which use sophisticated machinery to produce specialized goods, either alone or (frequently) in association with other small firms.

During the 1970s, groups of small firms of this type had been formed with extraordinary rapidity in the Third Italy. In the 1980s, despite the lack of systematic data on the organization of small firms in general, there was ample evidence that these systems now played a more important role in the advanced industrial economies than they had in the past. And there was also direct evidence that small firm systems were extraordinarily adaptable – at least partly because they collectively equipped themselves with services similar to those provided by large firms for their operational units, or because they integrated themselves into systems co-ordinated by the large firms, or for both these reasons.

A study by Perulli (1989) of the Modena area showed clearly that neither wage increases, nor Italy's entry into the European monetary system (which restricted opportunities for off-setting high production costs by devaluing the lira), nor the introduction of new microprocessor-based technologies had created insuperable barriers for the engineering firms in the area. Indeed, contrary to the predictions of many observers, the smaller companies fared better than the medium-sized ones. By contrast, a study by Trigilia (1989) showed that, in the Prato area, wage increases combined with a switch to a hard-currency regime and a shift in fashion away from the woollen goods typical of the area had disruptive effects, including the marginalization of the technically more backward sector of extremely small firms. But Trigilia's study also documented the amount of product and process innovations (especially the introduction of microelectronics) that enabled Prato to maintain its competitive edge.

In any case, there is substantial evidence of the convergence between large and small firms that we observed from the standpoint of the large firms. First, there was a growing tendency for consortia of small firms – acting either on their own or in association with public authorities and trade unions – to set up technical consultancies, training programmes and marketing agencies which supplied the same sort of services that (as we have seen) the large companies provided for their operating units. Whereas, until a few years previously, local governments in Italy had limited themselves principally to the provision of social services (canteens, day nurseries, public housing) and industrial sites, in the 1980s some of them began to collaborate in the delivery of the kinds of 'real' services that Montedipe, or the central offices at Falck or Italtel, provided for their respective operating units.

A good example of these developments is provided by the Centro Affari (Business Centre) created in Modena by the local government and Chamber of Commerce in response to demands by local firms for advanced services. The aim of this centre was to help firms apply flexible automation to their needs, export their products and adopt information technology. Prato also moved in this direction, as testified by the use of the Fondo per Interventi in Campo Sociale (a fund originally created by employers and unions to finance social services) to encourage structural adjustment through vocational training schemes and other projects and, even more clearly, by the efforts of the unions and employers' associations to secure regional legislation for the same purpose.

If flexibility is a precondition for success in a highly competitive environment, and if the reintegration of conception and execution is a precondition for flexibility, then, other things remaining equal, the kinds of changes I have described in corporate structure and subcontracting practices should have corresponded to analogous changes in the use of technology and labour on the factory floor. In Italy, in fact, the majority of large firms no longer rigorously applied mass-production principles to the organization of work and the use of technology. However, although some of them had obviously tried to break completely with these principles, others had equally obviously reorganized their plants in ways best interpreted as an adaptation of mass production.

An incontrovertible but nevertheless ambiguous finding is the widespread replacement of product-specific equipment with programmable machines, as well as efforts to teach workers a wide range of skills previously distributed among distinct categories of employees. The spread of flexible machinery was rapid in both small and large firms. Yet in some cases (e.g., Fiat and Olivetti) more recent machinery proved more rigid than the technologies used during the 1970s. Attempts to enlarge and recompose formerly distinct tasks were equally pervasive but equally ambiguous in their significance. At Montedison of Ferrara, there was a general flattening of factory-floor hierarchical levels; jobs were grouped into 'areas of integrated work'; and workers were rotated through a variety of jobs within the same installation, so that they could acquire and exercise broader skills and responsibilities. At Italtel, the aim was to train workers not only to operate and maintain several different machines, but also to check the quality of their output. Wherever possible, moreover, the aim was to organize workers into semiautonomous work groups with sufficient technical training to enable them to play an active role in organizing the flow of production in their area.

Fiat and Olivetti also trained machine operators to carry out a certain amount of preventive maintenance, set-up work and quality control. But these firms seemed more concerned to equip workers with the minimum of skills necessary to reduce down-time and scrap rates to acceptable levels than to provide them with the skills required to improve the organization of production as they progressively built up their experience of it.

Cases like Fiat and Olivetti can be explained in a straightforward way if one accepts the possibility that certain large firms decided to adopt a mixed strategy which deliberately combined features typical of mass production with others specific to flexible specialization, thereby creating a hybrid which might prove more effective than either of them. According to this explanation, these firms are not exceptions in an economy moving towards flexible specialization; they are, rather, the pioneers of a new strategy which one might call 'neo-Fordism' or 'flexible mass production' (Arrighetti 1988; Boyer 1988).

The aim of this strategy has been to increase product variants without abandoning the distinction between conception and execution. The corporation still believes it can predict demand. Instead of equipping itself to deal with unpredictable changes, and therefore reorganizing itself in order to make permanent reorganization possible, it simply tries to adapt to wider market fluctuations than have been the case in the past. Certain supervisory functions are eliminated at corporate headquarters, but the operating units – even if they are consolidated according to product line and administratively autonomous – are still regarded as divisions of the parent company, not as independent firms. Programmable automation makes it possible to reap the same benefits from the manufacture of a few closely related variants of a product as those yielded by dedicated equipment used to manufacture a single product. However, apart from some features such as computer-controlled tool changes, for example, a casual observer would not note any difference between the progress of an engine block along a line of programmable machine tools and its progress along a traditional transfer line of connected single-purpose machines. Workers are trained to operate the full range of new equipment so that they can easily switch jobs; but since the range of products is already well defined and the machines programmed accordingly, there is little incentive to teach them the basic principles of the new technology. The emphasis is instead on equipping workers with the knowledge and autonomy necessary to operate just-in-time delivery systems, which includes teaching them to detect defects and help to identify and eliminate their source.

Arguing that both further flexible specialization and a trend towards neo-Fordism are equally plausible scenarios is tantamount to saying that, even assuming that no major change occurs in the international economic system, the future of Italian industry is uncertain and will probably remain so for a long time to come. And if this is true with regard to the use of technology and work organization, it seems even more so with regard to personnel policies and industrial relations, to which I now turn.

THE COMPANY INVOLVEMENT OF WORKERS AND SECLUDED MICRO-CONCERTATION

It is fairly obvious that firms with different kinds of company and work organization tend also to adopt different models of personnel management and industrial relations. One might therefore also expect post-Fordist and post-Taylorist firms to manage human resources and trade-union relations in ways that differ markedly from those that used to predominate in Fordist firms. However, studies of various companies and industrial districts reveal that much more complex and contradictory processes are at work. These processes can be summarized as follows. First, new trends have indeed appeared, certain features of which are widespread and by no means confined to post-Fordist and post-Taylorist firms or to the more dynamic and innovative small-firm districts. Second, within these general trends, one conversely discerns increasing diversification, which prevents the elaboration of clear-cut typologies of personnel policies and of industrial relations.

I begin with the trends. In general, the available research – and not just in Italy – seems to indicate that, in the 1980s, the predominant trends in personnel management and union relations were the company involvement of the work-force and secluded micro-concertation.

By 'company involvement of the work-force' I mean all managerial efforts aimed at encouraging workers to identify closely with the company for which they work. Phenomena of this kind, and in general the enhancement of internal labour markets compared with the external labour market, were reported during the 1980s in such widely differing industrial systems as Germany's (Streeck 1984), Japan's (Dore 1986) and that of the United States (Kochan et al. 1986). The U.S. example, however, reminds us that managerial efforts to involve workers in production may aim exclusively at individuals, thereby replacing a system of industrial relations. In Italy, this strategy was by no means a novelty, since it had been typical of pre-Fordist (or semiartisan) production systems in the country and had been widespread even in Fordist firms, especially at the higher levels of the work-force (white-collar workers, technicians, skilled workers). Nevertheless, it was apparently not the predominant trend in Italy; indeed, the following phenomena were those most frequently encountered: the spread of quality circles and collective incentives tied to company productivity or to various indicators of company performance; sometimes union-backed group bargaining over production targets; various forms of company welfare; and schemes for professional upgrading and career development based on collective rules.

None of these phenomena was in itself entirely new. As continuous flow technologies became increasingly widespread in the early 1960s, a number of companies had already been experimenting with pay systems based on group bonuses, and this had led to a form of productivity bargaining involving the work team as a whole (Lutz 1975). What was indeed a novel feature, however, was the relatively general willingness of firms to accept the group dimension – collective rather than individual – in personnel management and incentive schemes, a willingness which, in the Italian case, almost always entailed firms' noninterference in trade-union action, if not their consent. Also relatively new was the trade unions' tacit acceptance, if not outright endorsement, of these developments.

Certainly, both case studies and quantitative surveys (Regalia and Ronchi 1988, 1989, 1990) show that direct and informal relationships between managers and workers also developed in many Italian companies. Nevertheless, these relationships did not come about in direct antithesis to collective bargaining or to traditional-style industrial relations. Instead, the two sets of relationships seemed to overlap peacefully, in the sense that there was coexistence, not interference, between them.

Furthermore, rather than generate direct individualized bargaining on wages and working conditions – as had always been the case for white-collar workers and as happened in nonunion U.S. sectors – in the 1980s the direct relationships between managers and blue-collar workers in Italian companies often took the form of group relationships centred on issues of productivity, career development and so on. In other words, corporate attempts to gain individual consensus seemed less widespread, while there was greater emphasis on providing various groups of workers with opportunities for discussion (often through channels made available by the unions), in order to achieve both consensus and technical inputs. This may also explain the frequent use of productivity-linked incentives, often group-based and backed by the unions.

The second trend – secluded micro-concertation in order to make work rules more flexible – was reported and discussed in several countries (e.g., in the United States, where General Motors [Katz 1985] and Xerox [Cutcher-Gershenfeld 1991] were well-known cases), but especially in Italy, where the 1980s saw increasing co-operation between firms and unions and significant attempts to secure the joint regulation of certain aspects of labour flexibility. Unlike the period of centralized political bargaining (1977–84), in the latter years of the 1980s the concertation of decisions was often intense, but it occurred entirely at the micro-level and was tied to specific company or territorial features, not to general criteria (in this, Italy followed and even accentuated the more general trends discussed in Chapter 5).

It is not easy to find unambiguous indicators of this trend, precisely because the strategies involved were not explicit. The pattern that emerged was one of a wide-ranging search for mutually advantageous, as opposed to unilateral, solutions, or more simply one where each party concerned pragmatically adjusted to the needs of the other, often assigning bargaining a compensatory role. Studies of adjustment by large firms placed particular stress on such phenomena as the discussion or informal bargaining of innovations and the flexible interpretation of existing work rules or the creation of new, informal ones.

On the other hand, it was widely known (Piore and Sabel 1984; Trigilia 1986) that the propensity to define problems jointly and to search for mutually advantageous solutions, as well as pragmatic adaptation to the requirements of the opposite party, were traditional features of small-firm districts with strong subcultures. The cases of Prato and Modena, studied more recently by Trigilia (1989) and Perulli (1989), respectively, confirmed that flexibility and co-operation were so deeply rooted in the social fabric of these areas and so buttressed by trust relationships that they often appeared intrinsic to individual employment relationships, and therefore did not require institutional mediation by representation bodies. The crucial role of local actors (chambers of commerce, local interest organizations, local governments) was to provide adequate support for this trust-based system by encouraging its social reproduction and by providing the resources – such as local social services – which were necessary for its continued existence and at the same time frequently the object of bargaining. Yet in these cases, too, signs of change could be detected: in Prato, greater formalization of relationships with a tendency to fix flexibility within a negotiated framework; in Modena, a differentiation in the style and contents of industrial relations, which led to greater importance being attached to company specificity as opposed to previous territorial uniformity.

Here, too, the outcome was a certain amount of convergence between large companies and small-firm districts. It is difficult to assess to what extent this convergence was due to reciprocally imitative behaviour, or even to a conscious change of strategy by firms and unions in order to incorporate positive aspects from the different models. Whatever the case may be, the actual outcome was greater homogeneity or, better, lesser importance of the traditional large company/small firm antithesis in accounting for the diversification of industrial relations. The latter feature certainly appeared to be the dominant one, as I shall now seek to show, but the company size variable seems to have had relatively little influence on it.

Having given due prominence to these new developments, I should point out that diversification was a twofold process. First of all, regarding both personnel management and industrial relations, in most of the firms and small-firm areas for which information is available, certain elements of the new pattern seemed to combine with typical features of the old one. The above-cited indicators of new developments were robust enough to indicate a new general trend. But in a number of firms they were still too weak, perhaps too transitory, for a new type of personnel management and industrial relations to be identified alongside those that were already known. Moreover, some of these indicators were also to be found in otherwise traditional company contexts. The 1980s was a period of transition, the interpretation of which is not greatly helped by reasoning in terms of clear-cut typologies. What one finds instead is the spread of the pragmatic eclecticism in managerial policies for the regulation of labour that I discussed in Chapter 7.

Second, even if one were still to insist on identifying types of personnel management and industrial relations, it would be misleading, judging from the available data, to relate each of them to corresponding types of company and work organization. In the 1980s there was a pluralization of possible coherences, so to speak, between these strategic areas. That is to say, choices made in one area corresponded only tenuously to choices made in the other.

The processes discussed so far had this important consequence: far from cohering into a recognizable overall pattern, company-level industrial relations fragmented with such a wide range of nuances that they are, as I have said, extremely difficult to fit into clear-cut typologies. Certainly, we can dismiss as inadequate the simplistic dichotomy which has long dominated debate in Italy and which sets unilateral managerial action – as supposedly exemplified by the Federmeccanica (the engineering employers' association) model – against the participative system exemplified by the Protocollo Iri (a set of rules on industrial relations collectively bargained in Iri, the state-controlled industrial holding).

To conclude, analyses of company-level bargaining (Baglioni and Milani 1990), as well as sample-based surveys of firms (Regalia and Ronchi 1988, 1989, 1990) and case studies (Regini and Sabel 1989), all report the notable intensity and pervasiveness of formal and informal negotiation in Italian firms during the latter half of the 1980s, and often its rather consensual character. Why, one may ask, after the rigidities imposed by the unions in the 1970s and their weakening in the early 1980s, did the majority of employers not definitively break with previous rules? And why did the trade unions, for their part, behave in the work-place in a manner very different from that practised, or at least preached, at the national level?

A first answer to these questions lies in the nature of the control over work exercised by the Italian trade unions when their power was at its height. In the 1970s, so-called *controllo della discrezionalità padronale* (control of employers' discretionary powers) was achieved by means of continuous bargaining between supervisors and shop stewards, not by the creation – as in the United States – of a system of rules subsequently incorporated into the definition itself of jobs. As a (probably unexpected) consequence, opportunities to reorganize work were not constrained, in either the company's or the workers' view, by a pre-established set of detailed rules. Hence, as the shop stewards' bargaining power declined, employers were able to reorganize production without encroaching on the principles that structured company life.

There is, however, a second explanation, one which accounts for the behaviour of both actors and enables us to frame industrial relations – together with the logic governing the Italian political system until the early 1990s – within a more general interpretation of the Italian case (see Chapter 4). Put briefly, it may have been precisely the extraordinarily high and politicized level of overt conflict in Italy that persuaded the actors to adopt a day-to-day routine based on the accommodation and pragmatic co-operation required to avert paralysis. The centralization of formal industrial relations from the late 1970s onwards placed the national level constantly in the spotlight, so that it was the most visible level and the one to which the greatest symbolic value was attached. It was in this arena that adversarial behaviour, or at least a sharp distinction of roles, predominated, so that any attempt at concertation ran into serious difficulties (Regini 1987). But at the peripheral level, precisely because of its relative insulation from the centre and its consequent lack of symbolic force, in most cases it was possible to achieve co-operation pragmatically, and sometimes to pursue objectives in the interests of both workers and employers. In the large companies, therefore, forms of micro-corporatism arose which would have been unthinkable in the intransigent years of the 1970s. In the small-firm areas, co-operation followed a pattern of already proven success which has been aptly called 'neolocalism' (Trigilia 1986).

Whatever the most convincing explanation may be, it was not necessary for Italian employers to bypass the trade unions in order to increase the flexibility of production and work; instead, they were able to use the unions as agents of re-regulation. Proof of this is the intense company-level bargaining, both formal and informal, on all aspects of labour flexibility that has characterized recent years (Baglioni and Milani 1990).

THE ROLE OF INSTITUTIONS IN INDUSTRIAL ADJUSTMENT

So far, I have tried to identify the most general trends exhibited by the industrial adjustment strategies of Italian firms in the 1980s. But I have also tried to highlight the uncertainties, the contradictions, the plurality of options that led to the diversification of some company policies, on the one hand, and to a nucleus of commonly shared ones, on the other. I shall now seek to provide some explanation for this diversification of industrial adjustment processes, both among firms and (especially) among countries apparently faced by similar challenges.

First of all, a number of researchers view the diversification of company strategies as resulting from new information technologies. For example, an analysis of various case studies of new technological and productive environments concludes that radically different patterns of work organization – in terms of skills, the division of tasks and decisional roles and even the ergonomic aspects of the quality of work – may coexist (Butera 1987). This has prompted the hypothesis that 'the information revolution is a potent factor in the destructuring of organizations and of occupational roles; but their restructuring into new configurations is influenced instead by cultural, sociopolitical, educational, economic and institutional factors' (Reyneri 1988: 153). However, this emphasis on the impact of new technologies – on their capacity to destructure but not to restructure – does not adequately explain the appearance of a range of options with which to address the problem of regulating labour (i.e., of managing personnel and organizing industrial relations).

From this more general point of view, one can only say that the diversification of strategies between one company and another, and between the industrial system of one country and another, reflects the perception by the actors concerned that there is no longer 'one best way' to organize production, to manage the labour market and to regulate labour. It also reflects the increasing importance in strategic decision-making of local variables: the particular historical and institutional features of a firm or an area and their specific endowment of resources.

Of course, the importance of local variables has always been well known to researchers. But they have now become crucial with the demise of the previously hegemonic model of production (Fordism as an archetype) and of designs for macro-national standardization and control (Keynesianism and incomes policies as the centralized control of demand, the labour market and industrial relations). The fragmentary nature of post-Fordist systems and their irreducibility to a restricted set of types are features of transitional phases in which a new global model has not (yet) come to predominate – phases, indeed, in which actors are unsure as to what exactly constitutes a constraint to be eliminated or a resource to be utilized (Streeck 1987). A situation of this kind generates pragmatic and adaptive behaviour and an incremental learning process in which local variables are extremely influential.

If this argument is valid, it follows that placing the emphasis on processes of diversification by no means restricts analysis to a purely ex post description; rather, it highlights patterns that have theoretical significance, and it carries important implications for the predictability of actor behaviour. However, apart from these general considerations, explanation is still required as to why industrial adjustment in Italy took place earlier, and often with greater success, than in other countries with economies that, in the 1970s, were apparently more stable and capable of development.

In times of turbulence and volatile markets, precocious economic adjustment such as Italy was able to achieve is largely a matter of institutional good fortune. In such periods, firms tend to avoid making an already risky situation even more hazardous. Their first reaction is to cling to well-established practices and to tread well-beaten paths.

The most fortunate firms – although they are almost always unaware of their luck – are those operating in countries whose institutions induce them to seek solutions which fit well with the new economic environment (Piore and Sabel 1984). This is not to imply, though, that these institutions are more efficient in terms of a set of economic or value criteria, only that their operation is a constraint which proves (often unexpectedly) decisive in inducing innovative behaviour. The least fortunate firms are those whose institutions instead block successful adjustment.

In order to understand Italy's good fortune from this point of view, it may be helpful to compare its situation in the 1980s with that of two countries – Austria and the United States – in which, for opposite reasons, adjustment was long obstructed by the operation of their institutions.

Given Austria's organization and regulation of labour, it is difficult to account for its economic difficulties in the 1980s. At the work-place level, in fact, the Austrian institutional system seemed to have responded well to the constraints imposed by the new models of industrial organization. This was confirmed by the fact that the German system – which was very similar to the Austrian one in this respect – had indeed facilitated adjustment (Streeck 1984). But the Austrian economy, and the large state-owned firms which dominate it, suffered from the extraordinarily close ties between a highly centralized (both vertically and horizontally) trade-union movement, on the one hand, and a quasi-consociational political system, on the other. During the 1970s, this system had been the envy of the Western world. Centralized negotiation over wages, prices, and monetary and fiscal policy had kept inflation low and unit labour costs under control. Subsidies to the state-owned firms had enabled them to avoid layoffs and had consequently reduced the unemployment rate (Marin 1983; Katzenstein 1984; Scharpf 1984).

Yet the same complex network of alliances that made co-ordinated macroeconomic management possible obstructed the reorganization of firms into more flexible operating units, even when awareness of the need for such restructuring became general. Since the workers in the state-owned companies formed the core of the Austrian trade-union movement, defence of those firms assumed the symbolic value of the defence of the trade-union organizations themselves. And because the unions had extremely close ties with the parties at the local and national levels – and the parties acted in concert with one another – it proved rather easy to secure public support for the status quo.

In many respects, the situation of industrial relations in the United States during the same period was the direct reverse of Austria's (Kochan et al. 1986). The unions were politically isolated and often internally divided. However, the weakness of the trade unions did not in itself facilitate industrial adjustment. Indeed, it encouraged managers to adopt suboptimal strategies, and for two diametrically opposed reasons. First, firms that chose traditional strategies of price competition through low-cost mass production saw the unions' weakness as an opportunity to increase their competitiveness by cutting wages. Second, firms that were aware of the need for a radical change in production strategies, and in particular the more flexible use of more skilled labour, were tempted by the unions' weakness to accelerate these processes by managing them unilaterally. The temptation was all the greater because the U.S. industrial unions – in contrast to those in Austria (or Germany or Italy) – had since the 1930s developed forms of control over work based on complex systems of promotion and job protection, which defined a worker's career as advancement by seniority up a ladder of very narrowly defined tasks. Thus, from the point of view of the more innovative managements, the unions were not valid interlocutors, since they were committed to the defence of one of the elements of the institutional structure of the firm – the definition in extremely narrow terms of jobs – which was most in need of radical reform.

The result was that employers often tried to impose vaguely defined co-operative relationships by fiat, with the predictable outcome that many workers rallied around the now-weakened unions and their more traditional objectives of defending narrowly defined jobs. The cumulative effect of these processes was a long delay in restructuring and the reorganization of work, and numerous interruptions once the processes had gotten under way.

Compared with these two polar cases of difficult adjustment, the success of many Italian firms seems, with hindsight, almost preordained. First of all, apart from the period following the 'hot autumn' of 1969, the Italian trade unions never possessed anything like the combination of economic and political power that obstructed adjustment in Austria. But in contrast to the U.S. unions, neither were they so weak as to induce firms to bypass them and pursue unilateral cost-cutting strategies (although there were some attempts in this direction) with all the hostility of unpredictable outcome that these would provoke.

Second, the unions exercised their power in ways which, knowingly or otherwise, often facilitated the restructuring of firms. As I have already argued, the Italian trade unions did not seek control over work in the sense given to this objective by the U.S. labour movement (i.e., the definition of jobs). Instead, they tried, on the one hand, to use their bargaining power to attain economic and social policy objectives – sometimes ones with a close bearing on the functioning of the political and institutional system – objectives which at first took the form of the *lotta per le riforme* (struggle for social reforms) and culminated in the concertation experiments of the late 1970s and early 1980s. Inside the work-place they sought, on the other hand, not so much to control jobs as to change the organization of work – suffice it to mention the demands for job rotation, enlargement and enrichment, the creation of autonomous work groups and so on that became widespread during the 1970s.

Of course, these strategies encountered strong resistance. They had to be mediated in various ways with the positions of employers and the government, and they were redefined accordingly. But the characteristics they acquired as a result of this process were such that the Italian economy moved rapidly along the path of adjustment. For example, as the concertation of economic policies (and a leftward shift in political equilibria) seemed increasingly unrealistic, the unions were obliged to adjust their aim to the sectoral and local levels – as well as proposing the 'return to the company' that I have already discussed. But in doing so, they transferred to these levels the mix of ingredients typical of their strategy during the concertation period of the late 1970s and early 1980s: the priority given to objectives of control over economic processes, the implicit acceptance of the political exchange method and the internalization of the constraints imposed by the crisis.

At the sectoral level, this led to a widespread willingness to accept the consensual management of restructuring based on 'sector plans' such as those drawn up for the chemicals, car and textiles sectors. In some cases, for example the car industry, these sector plans failed to produce any significant results. But in others they were of considerable importance in co-ordinating action by firms, unions and the government at the national and sometimes local levels.

At the local level, various institutional factors combined to turn this into an arena of potential co-operation. In Italy, local union organizations had a long tradition of independent initiative, in which more radical pressures by certain occupational groups were absorbed into more complex mediation strategies. And the public institutions often possessed economic resources and legitimacy greater than or in addition to those of the national institutions. Although a mediation of interest at the regional level had not developed to the extent that one might have expected, the role of agreements and especially of informal interactions at the local level grew in importance and encouraged the spread of the micro-concertation aimed at the recovery and development of the local productive fabric that I have already discussed. The industrial districts remain the clearest and best-developed example of this local micro-concertation, but they are not unique cases in the Italian industrial panorama.

The 'struggle against Taylorist work organization' of the late 1960s and early 1970s also helped, albeit indirectly, to accelerate restructuring. Unlike certain U.S. unions, such as the United Auto Workers which set themselves similar goals, the Italian unions were not afraid that a more flexible system would blur job classifications and thereby undermine the foundations of their contractual relations with firms. Indeed, for certain sections of the Italian labour movement, the struggle for new work organization came to acquire symbolic value as the first step towards the construction of a more humane society. By themselves, these attempts of the late 1960s and early 1970s to change work organization had only marginal effects – although the fact that firms like Fiat, Olivetti and Alfa Romeo experimented in flexible automation and the relative reorganization of work earlier than their foreign competitors surely owes something to union pressure. However, an unforeseen and indirect effect of shop-floor campaigns was that they sensitized workers and activists to these issues, so that when in the 1980s an increasing number of firms were attracted by the idea of reorganizing work in order to regain efficiency, they found that important sectors of the labour movement were ready and willing to negotiate change.

This is certainly not to argue that Italian workers unreservedly approved of these new tendencies. The fact that the demise of Taylorism became in the 1980s as much a management as a union slogan is sufficient to raise doubts as to its real meaning. But it is nevertheless true that this objective's close association with union struggles of recent memory implied that Italian trade unionists were much more willing than those in other countries to view the reorganization of work as a new and potentially positive terrain on which to continue their 'contest against capital', and therefore to participate in this reorganization instead of opposing it as an unambiguous threat to their past conquests.

This explanation in comparative terms of Italian industry's success during the 1980s – an explanation almost entirely founded on differences in institutional context – is undoubtedly only a partial account of the phenomenon. But it serves to support the principal hypothesis of this book: namely, that since the crisis of the centralized political regulation of the economy, national economic performance has come to depend to a significant extent on social and institutional factors operating in more hidden and disparate ways, primarily at the local level and the company micro-level as the most important arenas of regulation.

Conclusion: the uncertain boundaries between macro and micro – the production of collective goods in the European economies

The model of the centralized and concerted political regulation of the economy discussed in Part I based its legitimacy and attraction on two presuppositions: (1) if left to itself, the market is able to ensure neither the production of socially desirable goods (such as full employment or income security) nor the production of 'collective goods' (Olson 1965) for its principal actors, that is, firms (goods such as the containment of inflation, the development of human resources and social peace);[1] (2) consequently, these goods should be the object of policies elaborated centrally by public institutions acting in accord with large interest organizations. The first of these assumptions has rarely been contradicted over the half century since the end of the Second World War during which we have seen the rise and decline of this model of regulation in the European economies. By contrast, the evident difficulties, limitations and contradictions of the second assumption have bred doubts among scholars and political actors alike.

Reactions to these difficulties have ranged from a revival of the ideology of the unregulated market, on the one hand, to repeatedly frustrated attempts to render public intervention more efficient, on the other. Only rarely has consideration been given to the hypothesis that the production of collective goods might be, under certain conditions, the outcome of processes different not only from the workings of the market but from intervention by public institutions and interest organizations at the central level – intervention deliberately designed to achieve this goal and which seemed the only possible alternative to the free market. The myth of central state co-ordination as the only way to give overall rationality to the economic system, as the only antidote to market anarchy, so profoundly conditioned Keynesian economic culture and European reformism that the possibility of regulating the economy through other mechanisms and processes was for long disregarded.

COLLECTIVE GOODS AND MICRO-REGULATION

Part II has shown that in some specific cases these processes have in fact managed to develop, processes which I have called the micro-social regulation of the economy – as opposed to the macro-political model of regulation discussed in Part I. The term 'micro-social' highlights two distinctive features of this model which differentiate it from the 'macro' one. The first is the peripheral nature of the sites (mostly firms) that have become crucial to the production of collective goods as compared with the centralization of the previous system. The second is the predominance of initiatives taken by social actors (associations, trade unions, management) as compared with political actors.

But this model also differs from the macro one in other ways. Specifically, the regulative outcome (i.e., the production of the collective good) does not stem directly from deliberate intervention by public and private actors. Instead, it is often the unplanned result of scattered processes and of limited and particularistic goals pursued by these actors, on the one hand, and the existence of institutions which indirectly induce these same actors to adopt certain behaviours and not others, on the other. Rather than consisting of direct intervention deliberately intended to produce the collective good, therefore, micro-regulation involves processes which we may call indirect and derivative. Public institutions, in particular, play a solely facilitative role, one which enables civil society – that is, actors such as interest associations and management – to regulate themselves. Depending on the circumstances, this role may consist of establishing the rules and external constraints under which private actors operate, or it may be restricted to creating a framework of conditions – namely, of economic or authority resources – which enables their self-regulation.

Even when the self-regulation of civil society is broader in scope, however, its capacity to produce collective goods is still based – as we shall more clearly see in the final section – on the existence of institutional arrangements which induce actors to take certain courses of action and not others, thereby directing them towards this end. As in macro-regulation, in micro-regulation collective goods are therefore not produced solely through the spontaneous consensus of social actors, nor are they simply the outcome of rational calculation by market participants. Although direct, deliberate and centralized regulation has proved increasingly ineffective for the production of collective goods, this does not mean that private contract, or culture, or enlightened-rational economic insight of social actors is sufficient for the purpose. In short, in analysing the forms of micro-social regulation as those probably most effective in producing diverse collective goods, one cannot neglect the role of the institutions and assume a voluntarist view of social order.[2]

It should be obvious from this discussion that these are scattered processes, ones difficult to capture and define with precision, and that sometimes it is even more difficult to identify the institutional conditions that make them possible. For this reason the literature has paid them less attention than it has devoted to large-scale regulatory processes at the macro-level. Yet without adequate analysis of these processes, it is impossible to understand how it could be possible for the production of collective goods to continue in Europe even after the apparent return to more deregulated economies.

The second part of this book has concentrated on the ways in which, during the 1980s, it was possible to produce one such collective good for firms – that is, co-operative industrial relations – which constituted an important factor in the capacity of national economic systems to adjust to market changes. This is a collective good for firms because a flexible and co-operative work-force increases their competitiveness and is a common interest. Although in some countries and industries management has tried to obtain this co-operation by establishing a direct relationship with workers, thus bypassing the role of their representatives, in most European economies the involvement to some extent of trade unions has appeared inevitable because they are still powerful enough or enjoy sufficient political protection to raise major obstacles if excluded from the process.

It could be objected that this is only partly a collective good in that co-operative relationships can be created in a firm without their necessarily extending to others. However, the industrial relations systems of most European countries tend to preserve a relatively unitary character, and the trade unions in particular tend to homogenize their behaviour and to generalize more advanced local experiences through national-level bargaining. If co-operation manages to mould the style of union action in a particular country, if it translates into an industrial relations system with co-operative features at the national level, then it will also benefit those firms which have not sustained the cost of its production or reproduction.

This cost consists essentially of the involvement of the work-force – that is, having workers and/or their representatives participate in production and organizational decisions – with the reduction of managerial discretionary powers consequent upon it. The risk, as with all collective goods, is that no firm will contribute voluntarily, and therefore that these goods will not be produced or reproduced unless the firm is coerced into doing so (e.g., by laws which oblige firms to inform and consult the workers' representatives). However, the processes of micro-social regulation discussed in Part II proved, in many cases, to be more effective than coercion.

In this concluding chapter it is not my intention to resume my analysis of how and to what extent relatively co-operative industrial relations emerged during the 1980s. I shall show instead, in the next two sections, how processes of micro-social regulation became crucial to the production of other collective goods as well: namely, the curbing of inflation and the development of human resources. In the final section I shall analyse the components of these regulation processes in all three cases of collective goods production examined, and I shall consider the institutional conditions that make them possible.

In illustrating the various ways in which the curbing of inflation and the development of human resources have come about in European countries, I shall dwell on aspects that the literature has tended to neglect because of its emphasis on traditional ones. My discussion of the development of human resources will centre on emerging general trends – bearing in mind, of course, the many differences among European countries – while my discussion of the containment of inflation, whose general features are better known, will focus on differences among these countries.

THE CONTAINMENT OF INFLATION

A low inflation rate can be viewed as a public good which concerns an entire society: a low cost of living is in the interest of all consumers, and it is not possible to exclude from this good those who have not helped to produce it. However, there are several causes of inflation, and this provokes conflicts among various social groups, each of which is interested in combating one cause but not another. These diverse causes include the 'excessive' growth of aggregate wages, which triggers wage-push inflation. Regulating this growth may or may not be in workers' common interest (Lange 1984b), but its containment is certainly a collective good for firms exposed to international competition, since wage growth pushes up their labour costs and – to the extent that they cannot transfer these costs to prices – reduces their competitiveness. As with other collective goods, however, the temptations of free-riding are strong, because those firms which have not helped to pay its costs cannot be excluded from the benefits of low inflation, and they may therefore continue to use incentives, higher-than average wages and forms of wage drift in general to regulate labour.

Since the 1960s, the curbing of wage-push inflation has been regarded as closely tied to incomes policies. The latter, it was presumed, required major efforts of persuasion and co-ordination by governments as well as the co-operation of interest associations; they were, therefore, both consensual and centralized (Ulman and Flanagan 1971). Furthermore, when towards the mid-1970s the concept of concertation achieved its fullest development, it was seen as the obvious institutional framework for such policies. Consequently, the two phenomena soon came to be regarded as overlapping, or as inextricably bound together (Panitch 1977; Cameron 1984; Flanagan et al. 1984; Tarantelli 1986).

However, whereas the consensual regulation of wage growth was an objective largely shared by European social and political forces, macro-national concertation was an instrument deemed necessary in the 1970s to achieve that objective though in many countries it stirred up a hornet's nest of problems and dissent. While – as I have argued on various occasions in this book – this instrument has declined in all European countries, its objective continues to be pursued in at least some of them, with greater or lesser success, through other processes and mechanisms. It is precisely on these processes and mechanisms – those which I earlier called 'indirect and micro-social regulation' – that the following analysis of the main European national experiences intends to shed light. The aim in particular will be to show how in Germany, and to a lesser extent in Italy, processes of indirect regulation which do not affect the autonomy and initiative of the social partners have brought a considerable degree of de facto co-ordination to wage dynamics, whereas the assignment of a pre-eminent role to state intervention in France and to tripartite concertation in Spain has not averted wage dispersion.

Discussion may conveniently begin with the central thesis of an important article by David Soskice (1990b).[3] Soskice argues against the conclusions of an influential work by Calmfors and Driffill (1988) by maintaining that national systems with a high degree of co-ordination of wage dynamics between companies and industries have proved those best able to contain inflation and unemployment. However, the degree of co-ordination of wage dynamics does not necessarily coincide with the degree of formal centralization of the bargaining institutions. Wage growth can be co-ordinated and controlled through centralized bargaining, but also in other more complex and subtle – though variously effective – ways. Rephrasing Soskice's thesis, we may say that when we examine how the industrial relations systems of the principal European countries actually work in practice, we discover various functional substitutes for concertation which are used to pursue objectives similar to those of traditional incomes policies and which generate different national styles of wage dynamics regulation.

Of course, these styles achieve differing degrees of success, and they raise problems of greater or lesser difficulty. The countries in which wage growth is more closely co-ordinated are, on the one hand, those with strongly centralized bargaining systems (Austria, Norway and Sweden) and, on the other, those (like Japan and Switzerland) in which bargaining is formally decentralized to the company level but in which either the central employers' associations or informal 'wage cartels' among large firms and industrial groups ensure a very high level of de facto co-ordination. Here, however, I shall examine only the major European countries: these are not equipped with institutional arrangements of sufficient strength to guarantee the co-ordination of wage dynamics, which is consequently entrusted to more complex informal mechanisms of variable effectiveness.

Of the five largest European countries, only Great Britain does not have, and never had at any point during the 1980s, either institutions or practices able to solve the problem of co-ordination. The country's bargaining system is highly fragmented (it has been calculated that fully 90 per cent of pay in the private sector is determined at the company level; Visser 1992); multi-employer bargaining is practically nonexistent; the co-ordination capacity of the peak trade unions and employers' associations is extremely poor, as evidenced by the number of unions affiliated with the Trades Union Congress: no fewer than eighty-eight, as opposed to the fifteen to seventeen unions in Austria and Germany (Visser 1992); and the government stubbornly refuses to intervene, even to provide guidelines, in bargaining between the two sides of industry. In short, the British system is bereft of any mechanism on which co-ordination of wage dynamics could be based, and it may therefore be omitted from comparative analysis.

Of the other largest European countries, Germany has the most stable and efficient, albeit apparently cumbersome, system (Streeck 1991; Jacobi et al. 1992). The German case has never lent itself to easy interpretation from within the neocorporatist framework. In fact, although many of the organizational and political preconditions for tripartite concertation exist, it has never developed to its fullest extent. Perhaps the principal reason is that Germany's voluntary system for co-ordinating wage dynamics, although laborious, has proved to be very stable and efficient, and has managed to avoid the problems that beset attempts at explicit concertation.

The German system's capacity to co-ordinate and contain wage growth relies on the pattern-setting role assigned to the first industry agreement to be renewed (usually, but not always, that of the metalworkers organized by the powerful IG Metall, whose contract is renegotiated annually and on a *Land* basis), which functions as a 'range-finder' for the others. The willingness of the other industrial unions and employers' associations not to diverge too markedly from the pilot agreement depends on both the widespread conviction that overstraining these practices would cause the system to break down, with unpredictable costs for everybody, and the ability of the trade union and employer peak organizations to steer the decision-making processes of their respective peripheries by resorting to persuasion and, when necessary, to incentives or sanctions (Hall 1994).

To complete the picture, though in very broad outline, some further features of the German system should be mentioned. First, company-level bargaining is narrowly constrained, especially regarding wages and related issues. In actual fact, a certain amount of diversification in both pay and norms is tacitly permitted at this level, but the notable expansion of company-level bargaining, which took place in Germany just as almost everywhere else in the 1980s, mainly concerned qualitative issues and did not have major implications for wage dynamics. Second, wage policy in the public sector largely follows that of the private sector: for blue collar and white-collar workers the same system of de facto coupling to pilot agreements operates, and *Beamte* (civil servants) normally receive by law the average level negotiated for the former. Government and Parliament therefore have extremely limited discretionary powers and few opportunities to guide overall wage dynamics.

In conclusion, the co-ordination of wage growth in Germany is a rather orderly though complex process which involves a plurality of social actors situated between the centre and the periphery of the system and which functions because it rests on certain institutional underpinnings. Principal among these is the Bundesbank, which, since 1974, has overtly used its complete autonomy in monetary policy to influence annual wage bargaining (Scharpf 1991; Streeck 1994). Second, the law prescribes in detail the procedures and competencies pertaining to the various levels at which social actors interact (Thelen 1991; Turner 1992). Finally, central trade-union and employer associations have the ability to provide guidance based on the organizational structure and backed by incentives and sanctions (Soskice 1990b). With the passage of time, this institutional underpinning has produced in the social partners something akin to the internalization of shared imperatives sufficient to avert conflict – conflict which, when it emerges, may be as long and bitter as it was in 1992.

Regarding Italy, it is widely believed (see, e.g., Faustini 1990) that an incomes policy functioned more or less successfully during the period (1977–84) of macro-concertation, which was informal at first and then took the form of tripartite agreements (Regini 1987) and that, thereafter, wage growth was left to the market with no further attempts at control or overall co-ordination, until a new tripartite agreement in 1993 reinvented the incomes policy. In actual fact, more detailed analysis shows that some co-ordination of wage dynamics did take place in Italy, both in the period 1977–84 and subsequently, but by means of indirect and therefore less visible mechanisms.

Mention should first be made of the role played by the wage-indexation mechanism (*scala mobile*). With a degree of automated cover which, for the metalworkers, oscillated until the mid-1980s around 80 per cent (ASAP 1989), the negotiable margins of wage growth – and therefore of wage diversification – were extremely narrow, and all the industrial unions were able to set adequate restraints on their wage claims. Second, even after the substantial scrapping of index-linking mechanisms, co-ordination of wage growth continued, in the industrial sector, to be ensured by the de facto leadership assigned to the industry agreements for the metalworkers. These contracts tended to ensure a minimal basis common to all workers rather than strongly incremental objectives. De facto, they remained in effect for four years and wage increases were staggered over this period. Most nonpay issues were referred to company-level bargaining, which thus tended to concentrate predominantly on these matters and largely de-emphasized its supplementary role in wage negotiations.

In addition to these important wage co-ordination mechanisms, in certain periods there may have been other, more variable effective ones at work. Soskice (1990b), for example, attributes considerable importance to the following features: the links among the largest Italian firms and between these and the banking system, links which have enabled them to act in a co-ordinated manner; the attempt by IRI (a holding of state-controlled companies) to develop coherent pay strategies among the firms belonging to the group and the close supervision of company-level wage negotiations by the larger regional employers' associations.

Hence in Italy, too, some indirect mechanisms for the consensual control of wage dynamics have been in operation – mechanisms which are based on the existence of specific institutions and which involve social actors situated between the centre and the periphery of the system. Certainly their degree of stability and efficiency is not comparable to Germany's, mainly because certain crucial features of the German system of co-ordination are absent in Italy. The most important difference between the two systems is the possibility of co-ordination between the public and private sectors of the economy. Among other things, because of the large number of *Beamte,* who are excluded from negotiation, the wage dynamics of the public sector in Germany largely follow those of the private sector. In Italy, by contrast, the public sector has long represented the major obstacle against a wage restraint policy designed to lower the inflation rate. The recent law on the privatization of the employment relationship in many public services may help to solve the problem by linking public-sector wage increases more closely to those in sectors exposed to international competition.

Turning to the French system, we find that this too is less efficient than Germany's and that, furthermore, it resembles to a much lesser extent a model of micro-regulation than either the German or the Italian case. Paradoxically, the devices employed to achieve a certain co-ordination of wage dynamics are precisely those which most markedly differentiate it from the two earlier cases: namely, the governments's strong activism and active interventionism, and the extreme weakness of the trade unions (Goetschy and Rozenblatt 1992). Macro-national tripartite concertation has never got off the ground in France either, despite a timid attempt by the Socialist government in 1981–2.

However, there are numerous political and 'top-down' mechanisms, both direct and indirect, for determining wage levels. Direct mechanisms include the SMIC (minimum guaranteed wage) and, in general, measures introduced by the government to protect low-wage-earners – measures which have had a certain influence on small-firm sectors and have impeded excessive downward pressure on wage levels. More important, however, has been indirect government intervention on pay-related issues, which I can describe here only in outline form. By exploiting the existence of a vast public sector, especially since the nationalization of large industrial companies in 1981–2, the French government has geared wage dynamics closely to the objective of reducing the inflation rate, so that pay restraint has consequently predominated. These dynamics have been largely followed in the private sector, not because of the presence of strong interest associations with a certain ability to direct the entire process as in Germany, but on the contrary because of the extreme weakness of the French trade unions (indicative of which is the slump in trade-union membership to below 10 per cent; Visser 1992), which has prevented them from independently extracting concessions greater than those deriving from government action.

The French bargaining structure is not as orderly and rational as the German (Money 1992). There are first of all *interprofessionélles* (economy-wide) agreements, which in the 1980s were important with regard to qualitative issues. Few of these agreements concerned wages, however, and two of the main unions, CGT and Force Ouvrière, regularly refused to sign them. There is, then, the industry bargaining revived by the government as part of its campaign to raise low wages in the private sector. Finally, there is company-level bargaining, which in France as well appears today more significant than it was at the beginning of the 1980s.

These features of the system explain why, despite government efforts to assign the role of wage leader to the public sector, wage differentials between the private and public sectors have widened to the advantage of the former (Marsden and Silvestre 1990). This demonstrates the ineffectiveness of a system based mainly on government intervention to curb overall wage dynamics. Its weakness is an inability to build the strong and stable relationships between the social partners that would lend predictability to the system. This inability stems in equal measure from the employers' associations' reluctance to enter such relationships and from the weakness and division of the unions – which, moreover, have never developed a culture of economic compatibilities.

Finally, the Spanish case shows the inadequacy of a system for determining wage dynamics in which, for most of the 1980s, a central role was officially assigned to tripartite concertation. The superficial impression of the Spanish case is one of a highly juridified and centralized system (Valdés Dal-Ré 1991) in which macro-national concertation played a key role in co-ordinating wage dynamics and, in general, actors' behaviour (Pérez-Díaz 1987; Ojeda Avilés 1990; Espina 1991; Roca 1991). However, closer examination reveals that the situation is rather different today (as, indeed, it was in the 1980s). Whereas the juridification of the Spanish industrial relations system is effectively quite high, its centralization did not greatly affect bargaining practices, which continue to be fragmented and produce more dispersion than co-ordination (Ruesga 1991).

Bargaining over wages can take place at both the industry and company levels. Industries with bargaining autonomy are numerous in Spain and coincide with very specific branches. Depending on existing traditions, industry agreements may be signed at the national, regional or provincial level, the most typical form of wage negotiation being branch negotiation at the provincial level. But contrary to the German case, the industry-level actors which bargain first do not do so after a lengthy process of mediation internal to the employers' and trade-union associations, and they thus do not set a pattern for the others. The stronger industries and firms pay scant attention to the need for overall co-ordination of wage dynamics, and this gives rise to a dangerous degree of fragmentation and imitation. What makes the Spanish system so resistant to centralized regulation, despite almost a decade of macro-national concertation, is above all the weakness of interest organizations, which have very few incentives and sanctions at their disposal with which to control behaviour at the periphery of the industrial relations system. The unions represent around 15 per cent of the labour force; they do not have selective incentives to offer to their members; and they are often internally divided (Miguelez 1991). The employers' confederation is especially weak, and the industrial associations, although stronger, reflect an industrial structure essentially polarized between a handful of multinational corporations and myriad small firms. Despite the efforts of a government inspired by the activism of its French counterpart, the institutional conditions to render co-ordination of wage dynamics really effective are lacking.

To conclude this cursory review of the principal European cases, one may observe that co-ordination and consensual containment of wage dynamics have been efficiently achieved in Germany, and a little less efficiently in Italy, by reliance on indirect, noncentralized, regulatory mechanisms largely based on initiative by the social partners. They have functioned less well in France and Spain, where direct public regulation or centralized concertation has maintained a pre-eminent role. Although a certain laboriousness, and in some cases the precariousness connected with regulatory processes based on the initiative of nonpublic and noncentral actors, have been evident, we may conclude that the objectives traditionally assigned to incomes policies have been shown to be viable even without state intervention and without resorting to the classic instrument of macro-national concertation.

THE DEVELOPMENT OF HUMAN RESOURCES

In recent years, a number of European sociologists and economists have directed their attention to training policies and the availability of skilled labour as a crucial factor in the competitiveness of a national economic system (Maurice et al. 1982; Soskice 1990a; Dore 1987; Streeck 1989). Streeck, in particular, makes the strongest claim for the key importance of human resources. His analysis may be summarized – at the price of a certain amount of simplification – as follows. The competitiveness of a national economic system with high wages and a well-developed welfare system can be maintained only if its firms are equipped to compete not on prices but on quality. However, a production model of this kind requires a work-force that is not only highly skilled but also broadly skilled, with basic theoretical training closely tied to the work experience. This result can best be achieved by a system of vocational training like Germany's: a 'dual' apprenticeship system which provides training partly within the firm and partly outside, and which equips a large section of the labour force with high and broadly based skills.

However, although firms may gain a competitive advantage from this ample availability of human resources, they are induced to resort to 'free-riding', in the sense that they let other firms carry the training costs and then 'poach' their newly qualified workers – which they are able to do because these workers possess general, not firm-specific, skills. A highly and broadly skilled work-force is a classic collective good for firms, with all the well-known problems that it entails. In order to avoid free-riding, therefore, a system of vocational training of this kind must be highly institutionalized and guaranteed by the law and strong trade unions which oblige firms to pursue their long-term interests – thereby also acting for the general good of society (Streeck 1984).[4]

This argument – that institutions are required to constrain the market to produce those positive outcomes that its participants, as rational actors, would be unable to produce – may be attractive from an analytical standpoint. However, it belongs to that overly rigid view of the possible ways in which collective goods can be produced – a view which this book, and this chapter in particular, aims to replace with a broader and more articulated one which also assigns a role to peripheral, indirect, nonpublic mechanisms in such production. One must establish whether there are alternative solutions to the model of a state which obliges firms to concur in the production of the collective good – situations, that is, in which the production of this good is the outcome of scattered processes activated by peripheral actors indirectly motivated by a favourable institutional framework. The conviction that such situations not only exist but are acquiring crucial importance for human re-sources development derives from a heterogeneous corpus of research find-ings[5] which indicate the recent emergence of a number of general trends that in large measure are common to firms in various European countries.[6]

The first of these trends can be summarized thus: a number of firms tend to regard internal training for newly hired workers and further training for their employees as even more crucial than vocational training before entry into the labour market. There are various reasons for this. Because of the general increase in educational levels, even when firms are recruited for relatively low-skilled jobs, they are able to draw on a reservoir of post–mandatory school leavers (and even university graduates) who have already received basic theoretical training and require only specific on-the-job instruction. Moreover, because of changes in production systems, firms need work-forces which are closely involved and identified with the company. The further training of their employees therefore assumes a role and a symbolic content which go beyond the simple requirement of mastering technological innova-tions.

These developments have major implications for training. In fact, the suc-cess of the internal training of new employees and of further training obvi-ously depends to a far lesser extent on the efficiency of public training institu-tions. Decisive instead, for large firms, becomes the organization of the firm itself as a learning system: with incentives and career paths, use of internal labour markets, the ability of line management to teach rather than merely control and the formal recognition of implicit training functions (flanking). For small firms, the good functioning of firm networks and the creation of private–public training consortia are of major importance (Brusco 1986).

The second trend can be outlined as follows. Individual technical-professional skills have become relatively less important, whereas collective technical and social-relational skills (such as co-operation in problem-solving and an ability to work with others and to take the initiative) are today crucial. The reasons for this lie in the rapid adjustment to the market and the constant reorganiza-tion required of firms wishing to compete on international markets. This requirement has led, in industrial firms, to the spread of teamwork, or at any rate to forms of work in groups, which require relational abilities. It has, moreover, shifted the attention of firms to projects for total quality manage-ment, for lean production, and so on, which require precisely these abilities and in large measure. In service firms, the extraordinary growth of product sales and customer relations functions compared with administrative ones has rendered demand for social-relational skills almost as impelling as that for sufficiently broad technical knowledge.

The implications of this development converge with those already discussed. For firms, even more decisive than vocational training in the strict sense become policies designed to enhance worker identification and involvement with the company, the issue of how to teach and transmit the corporate culture to its workers, the identification of facilitative or obstructive institutions and mechanisms. Moreover, with regard to internal training, the more or less hierarchical manner in which work is organized has become more important than the expansion of training activities in the strict sense.

This brings us to the third general trend. Skilled production workers – who used to be the principal targets of traditional training schemes – have now become less essential for successful company performance, while the skills development of middle management, on the one hand, and of sales and external relations personnel, on the other (for small firms, the training of the entrepreneur him- or herself), are now crucial. In fact, several of the tasks traditionally performed by skilled and semiskilled workers (and by the administrative staff) have been made redundant by technological innovation. More important, however, production functions have progressively lost their central importance and their place has been taken by marketing ones.

Here, too, the implications appear largely to coincide with those already discussed. What is most required of these occupational groups is not specific knowledge but the ability to assume responsibility and to co-ordinate others, as well as general knowledge about the external environment and a flair for social relationships (with customers and colleagues). However, it appears that no truly satisfactory solution has been found to the problem of how these qualities can be taught and transmitted, and which institutions and mechanisms are facilitative or obstructive to this end. The German dual system has been reformed to incorporate the transmission of social skills, but the effectiveness of such reform has yet to be put to the definite test. In the other European countries, one notes a response by private or public actors which is for the moment sporadic and poorly structured – a sure sign of the existence of the problem but not necessarily a stable and satisfactory solution to it.

The fourth trend is closely tied to the others. Of apparently decreasing importance are formal mechanisms for training workers in a task or a technique. It is more crucial to provide indirect and continuous opportunities for workers to learn how to redefine their work flexibly according to the changing requirements of the market – that is, the informal and incremental training which goes by the name of 'learning by doing'. This appears to be generally true for large firms, and not solely with regard to the occupational groups, types of skills and training stages that, as we have seen, are now becoming of central importance; to some extent this pattern extends to traditional production workers, to the acquiring of individual technical skills and to the initial stage of training as well.

The consequences of the process are, for large firms, a tendency to internalize training processes. But even more important becomes the ability, or lack of it, of these firms to promote self-directed learning. This ability is necessarily connected to the way in which work is organized, to the functions of the company hierarchy and to the incentives system used by the firm.

Finally, many of the European firms for which relevant information is available seem to resort increasingly to their internal labour markets to fill skilled job vacancies; and, conversely, they rely increasingly less on direct hiring in the external market. An important consequence of this tendency is that the risks of free-riding are significantly reduced; that is, firms are less reluctant to make major investments in training for fear that once their workers have developed their skills, they will be poached by rival firms offering higher wages because they have not had to meet the costs of training. Consequently, firms have a greater incentive to give specialized training or retraining to their work-forces, and with the focus on the identification-building functions of such training – that is, on imparting symbols and messages to workers which induce them to identify more closely with the company.

The general trends discussed here therefore seem to lead to a relatively unambiguous conclusion. In the advanced European economies characterized by the diffusion of post-Fordist production regimes, the development of the collective good 'availability of properly skilled human resources' is likely to depend more on what happens within the firm than on the efficiency of the public training institutions external to it.

Of course, this is not to imply that an efficient public training system will not continue to exert a major influence on the competitive capacity of a country. Nevertheless, the ability of company supervisors to teach and of the organization of the firm itself to function as a learning system, the existence of internal and external social relations which are co-operative enough to allow for workers' involvement in their company and the presence of trade unions and industrial relations which favour the revision of rules for this purpose while preventing changes which devalue human resources become factors just as crucial as an efficient basic training system. The way in which the micro-regulation of human resources at the level of the firm – that is, the informal, decentralized and nonpublic mechanisms by which these resources are produced and managed – takes place appears in many respects to be even more decisive than the public institutions external to the firm that have traditionally catered to its training needs.

THE FEATURES AND CONDITIONS OF THE
MICRO-SOCIAL REGULATION OF THE ECONOMY

Having illustrated the various ways in which collective goods for firms – namely, co-operative industrial relations, co-ordination of wage dynamics and human resources development – are produced in the European economies, I can now return to a more analytical examination of the processes of micro-social regulation that generate them. The discussion of collective goods has confirmed that these processes display three principal features:

1. They are peripheral and relatively dispersed, in the sense that the sites on which collective goods are produced are decentralized, distant from the centre of the regulation system and not necessarily co-ordinated among themselves.
2. The initiative is taken principally by social actors rather than political ones, in the sense that the former are the protagonists, the subjects upon whose behaviour the production of the collective good crucially depends, despite the frequent presence of public policies explicitly designed for this purpose but of scant practical effectiveness.
3. The regulation process is indirect. Unlike public policies aimed directly and deliberately at the regulatory outcome, social actors direct their behaviour towards particularistic goals, and they are normally indifferent as to whether such behaviour happens to coincide with the production of collective goods. The latter, consequently, is often only an unintended consequence of the former.

However, the examples of collective goods analysed have confirmed that they are not produced spontaneously as the straightforward outcome of rational calculation by actors, or of their culture or tradition, or of a natural consensus. The pre-existing arrangements and institutions are decisive, albeit indirectly, in the sense that they are conditions which shape the behaviour of social actors.

These features and institutional conditions of micro-social regulation are exhibited very clearly in the production of those collective goods analysed in Part II and in this concluding chapter.

1. The availability of a work-force able and willing to co-operate in the goal of industrial adjustment has, in all European countries, resulted from a mix between state labour policies and the formal and informal involvement of workers in their companies. In more recent years, however, the importance of the latter vis-à-vis the former has grown to the point that it is now decisive. In no major European country, with the partial exception of France, has the adjustment of national productive systems to changes in the market been to a significant extent the outcome of government intervention targeted to this end. Adjustment has instead been the aggregate outcome of processes operating at the level of the firm. These processes may be characterized as the de facto joint management between employers and workers' representatives

which occurred in numerous companies during the phase of organizational restructuring and which has often persisted since then in the form of a permanent search for greater flexibility and improved quality.

With regard to the containment of inflation, too, the predominant instrument of the 1970s – concerted incomes policies – has played a secondary role, if one excludes the early 1980s in Spain. The crucial processes in the production of this public good have in many countries been industry-level collective bargaining – whether at the national or subnational level – combined with formal or informal mechanisms of co-ordination, adaptation or imitation among industries and among firms. This, therefore, is a type of consensual control of wage dynamics brought about not by central actors but by a plurality of actors whose behaviour may or may not converge towards the same goal.

Finally, the development of human resources appropriate to advanced economic systems is certainly still determined more by public policies – that is, by the operation of training institutions – than are the other collective goods I have considered. Nevertheless, we have seen the extent to which on-the-job training or further training within firms is expanding and increasingly covers the training needs of companies. We have also seen the growing contribution to the enhancement of human resources made by self-directed learning, by employee involvement policies and by supervisors motivated less to control than to teach. In this case too, therefore, peripheral and scattered processes perform a role that is tendentially more crucial than that of traditional training schemes.

2. The key actors in building co-operative industrial relations have undoubtedly been company management, on the one hand, and company-level workers' representatives, on the other. It is impossible (as is implicit in the foregoing discussion) to assign a protagonist's role to either public authorities or to national-level employers' and trade-union associations. The latter, in fact, have performed more passive and low-profile roles, often letting matters take their course without intervening, and even at times seeking weakly to oppose the processes taken place in firms.

Employers' and trade-union associations have instead played a leading part in the co-ordination and containment of wage dynamics – albeit more in Germany than in Italy, and more in these two countries than in Spain and France. In the first two countries, in fact, besides being the actors in industry-level bargaining, these associations have performed a major role, more or less effectively, in intraorganizational co-ordination – that is, in convincing their members to conform with the strategies adopted, in resolving internal conflicts and in pre-mediating among demands.

Finally, with regard to further training and on-the-job training, as well as the modes of employee involvement and the organization of work now making an increasing contribution to the overall production of human resources, the protagonists have obviously been firms themselves. However, small firms – which do not have the resources to provide their own training – must rely on networks or consortia among firms and their associations, chambers of commerce or universities and therefore on a plurality of private and public actors acting in coordination.

3. Empirical research shows that only in extremely rare cases have firms involved workers' representatives in productive processes or invited them to manage restructuring jointly as a conscious and long-term strategy, with the objective, that is, of consolidating a culture of co-operation and flexibility among the work-force which favours adjustment. Employers have pursued much more limited objectives, usually seeking to avoid conflict during the innovation and restructuring phases in which they are most vulnerable and to obtain benefits from the public institutions by exploiting the residual degree of legitimation enjoyed by the unions (see Chapter 7). Their introduction of employee involvement and de facto joint management has almost invariably been grudging, although it has triggered a learning process which has led many employers to appreciate the advantages of the consensual increase in work-force flexibility. Workers' representatives accepted micro-concertation mainly because of their need to preserve recognition by firms at a time of adverse power relationships. This acceptance was therefore pragmatic and instrumental in spirit; it did not imply a commitment to a co-operative model of industrial relations.

As far as the curbing of wage dynamics is concerned, employers' associations have performed their variably patient and effective work of intra-organizational co-ordination less to keep the inflation rate under control than to pursue more particularistic interests: rendering the growth of labour costs predictable, keeping differences among firms and industries within acceptable limits and, above all, reaffirming by this means their role vis-à-vis their members. The trade unions, for their part, have found in the intra- and intersectoral co-ordination of wages an ideal opportunity to exploit situations in which they are organizationally strong in order to tide them over situations in which they are weak.

Finally, firms engaged in on-the-job and further training, or those which have adapted work organization in order to offer opportunities for self-learning or to change the role of the company hierarchy, do not pursue collaboration with public training institutions in order to raise the skills level of the work-force. They seek instead to prevent the poaching of their workers by rival firms by teaching them more specific skills which are not easily sold externally. At the same time they look for opportunities to impart that identification with the company and that 'sensitization' to its goals which cannot be furnished by public training bodies.

Therefore, in none of the cases examined is the production of the collective good the direct result of action deliberately undertaken for this purpose. It is instead a secondary and fortunate effect of actions directed towards particularistic ends. However, even though this effect is unintended, it is not accidental. It is produced only under institutional conditions which induce actors to behave in certain ways and dissuade them from behaving in others.

For instance, firms sought co-operative industrial relations to manage industrial adjustment and to achieve flexibility, (a) the more the legal and political framework in which they operated made the alternatives more costly, (b) the more they had to deal with strong unions, able to render unilateral strategies expensive and at the same time embedded in a co-operative tradition (as in Germany) or in a productivist culture (as in Italy; see Chapter 8) and (c) the more they could count on incentives, resources and infrastructures provided by public institutions, ones which were usually not created deliberately in order to favour adjustment but already existed.

Moreover, the possibility of containing wage dynamics depends, as we have seen, first and foremost on the co-ordination capacity of interest associations, which is in turn a function of the way in which they are organized, of the powers granted to them by the law and so on (Swenson 1989; Golden 1993). Equally important is a bargaining structure which prevents free-riding leading to wage drift – one, that is, in which it is clearly specified who can bargain about what and following what procedures, so that it is impossible, for instance, to use company-level bargaining to bypass rules on wage increases set at the national level. The German case, moreover, has highlighted the extraordinary importance that may attach to public institutions when they do not seek to regulate wage dynamics directly but instead restrict themselves to influencing the behaviour of the social partners by indirect means.[7]

Finally, the probability that firms will develop training schemes which are different from traditional ones but which nevertheless end up performing a role just as important as that of public training bodies depends on at least two institutional conditions. The first is the existence of a school system which provides a basic theoretical-technical education of sufficient breadth and versatility that the more specific training provided by the firm can be efficiently grafted onto it. The second is the existence of local governments, chambers of commerce and other institutions able to create networks and consortia providing training in all cases when firms lack the resources to do so by themselves.

So institutions perform a role in the micro-social regulation of the economy that is just as important as their role in macro-political regulation: they indirectly shape the behaviour of actors by offering incentives to follow certain courses of action and disincentives against following others. To what extent micro-regulation processes will become an effective alternative to macro-regulation in the production of other public goods is, as I have said, difficult to predict. The boundaries between micro and macro, between their respective ranges of action, are still uncertain. But if macro-political regulation contin-ues to be scaled down in favour of micro-social regulation, this will not necessarily mean – as I hope to have shown – the increasing irrelevance of institutions and the greater weight of the deregulated market in determining economic outcomes.

Notes

Introduction

1. As noted by Lange and Regini (1989). Some of the following pages in this introduction, as well as the first section of Chapter 3 and the second section of Chapter 4, draw freely on this book.

2. Unstable concertation

1. The literature on these phenomena abounds. The reference texts are the collections of essays edited by Schmitter and Lehmbruch (1979), Berger (1981), Lehmbruch and Schmitter (1982) and Goldthorpe (1984). A large number of authors have also sought to define and distinguish the two concepts (see, e.g., Regini 1982). For the purposes of my present discussion, however, I shall treat them as synonymous.
2. Moreover, the hierarchy of the successful countries changed during the 1980s, and the relation between good performance and the presence of neocorporatist arrangements was therefore disputed even by scholars more favourable to the latter (Soskice 1990a).
3. Obviously, we should examine the strategies of the two main organizations usually involved in concerted policy-making: trade unions and employers' associations. My analysis, however, considers only the former, both for the sake of brevity and because too little information or analysis is available concerning the latter for generalizations to be made. Swenson (1989), who has written one of the very few comparative studies of the strategies of employers' associations (in Sweden, Denmark and Italy), criticizes this shortcoming, without bearing in mind, however, that it is unwise to discuss the action of subjects when one knows very little about them.
4. The following account draws largely on Regini (1984).

3. Organized interests and public policies

1. This typology differs somewhat from that set out in the introduction to Lange and Regini (1989). The additional empirical evidence gathered in the meantime has persuaded me to revise our description of each of the types proposed.
2. However, this delegation is granted only to certain organized interests endowed

with sufficient resources. Thus, the minimum of insulation against these interests coincides with maximum of insulation against all others – that is, with the exclusion of the latter.

3. See, e.g., Richardson (1982) for the first concept (policy community) and Heclo (1978) for the second (issue network or policy network), which I shall use in my discussion here. I thank Gloria Regonini for having drawn my attention to the differences between the two concepts – differences which have persuaded me to use the latter.

4. Note that oligopolistic bargaining practices usually involve the externalization of the costs incurred in reaching agreement onto actors excluded from the decision process. This may destabilize this type of policy-making should the groups excluded from it manage to organize themselves and apply pressure on the decision process.

5. For instance, it is highly unlikely that bureaucracies or fragmented interest groups would be able to dominate oligopolistic bargaining or that large encompassing organizations could dominate pluralistic pressure/spoils system governance.

6. A number of concepts widely current in political science seem to suggest the opposite, however. Party government, bureaucratic government, the colonization of the state by private interests and iron triangles or stable alliances among certain of these actors are often proposed as models for the entire decision process.

7. The distinction between the two stages of policy formation and policy implementation is partly an arbitrary one, as public-policy analysts frequently remind us. However, from the point of view of organized interests – their role, their strategies and the symbolic significance of their actions – establishing relationships with governments and parliaments is very different from establishing relationships with public administration bodies. Equally arbitrary is the view of public institutions as single-logic actors, since they in fact constitute arenas of encounter and conflict among many different actors. 'The [public] body . . . is no longer an entity but a market, or better still, a potential battleground for armies, divisions, companies, and sharpshooters, that is, for those groups . . . that open fire or negotiate, ally, and separate again' (Pizzorno 1981:262). Nevertheless, for the specific purposes of my analysis here, we may consider public institutions and organized interests to be collective actors, ignoring their differences and internal dynamics. In fact, my task is to identify certain ideal types of relationship – that is, stylized forms of interaction – which enable comparison among empirical cases and which, especially, show the specific effects of these relationships on the functioning of both public institutions and organized interests.

4. An anomalous case?

1. However, although this operation facilitates analysis, it may (as we shall see) impede solution of the apparent paradox I have referred to.

5. The crisis of political exchange and the growth of micro-concertation

1. Although an exception has been the tripartite agreement of July 1993 in Italy, signed after a decade of failed attempts at reaching an accord.

6. The search for flexibility

1. The first section of this chapter as well as Chapter 8 owe much to the ideas of Charles Sabel, since they are based on research directed jointly by us and drawn from our book summarizing its main results (Regini and Sabel 1989).

7. The problem of consensus in production

1. The enormous growth of interest in Total Quality Management, and more generally in the Japanese model of the organization of production (e.g., Womack et al. 1990), brought the question of consensus in production to the forefront.
2. Here the term 'regulation' has little to do with the French *régulation* school; nor does it carry the simplistic meaning of 'public intervention' ascribed to it in much of the economic literature. It is, moreover, employed in a way that differs slightly from the concept of 'forms of regulation' developed by political economy and used in the introduction to this book.
3. The following discussion is based on a comparative research study co-ordinated by the present writer and conducted in 1991–2 in fifteen industrial companies located in Italy, France, Germany, Great Britain and Spain (forthcoming). The research team consisted of Paolo Perulli and Ida Regalia (Italy), Alain Lipietz (France), Bruno Cattero (Germany), Paul Marginson (Great Britain) and Fausto Miguelez (Spain). In each country, case studies were made of companies in the chemical, food processing and engineering industries. Interviews were held with the company management as well as with workers' representatives and trade unionists. The research was funded by the University of Trento.
4. It should be stressed that the unions might favour or oppose change in certain aspects of the employment relationship because they themselves were uncertain how to react to managerial initiatives and how to assess their residual capacity to condition them.

8. An emblematic case

1. See note 1, Chapter 6. The analysis in this chapter relies heavily on Regini and Sabel (1983).

Conclusion

1. I discuss below the extent to which each of these represents a collective good in the sense given to the term by economic theory – that is, a good which corresponds to an interest common to the members of a group but whose enjoyment by some is inseparable from its enjoyment by others. Of course, this raises the classic problem of 'free-riding' – the problem that benefits accrue also to those who have not helped to pay the costs of the production, so that a rational actor is not normally motivated to contribute.
2. I wish to thank Wolfgang Streeck for having repeatedly called my attention to this point.

3. The analysis in this section draws on Soskice's arguments, which have been developed and modified on the basis of an empirical survey of four European countries co-ordinated by the present writer and conducted by Mimmo Carrieri and Ida Regalia.

4. An institutional alternative which moves in a similar direction might be seen in the French case, where the state obliges firms to invest a percentage of their wage costs in further training.

5. Including the preliminary findings of two research projects co-ordinated by the present writer: the first on Germany, Italy, France and Spain, the second on the so-called engine regions of these countries (Baden-Wuerttemberg, Lombardia, Rhône-Alpes and Cataluña). In both cases, expert informants were interviewed and case studies conducted of firms in the machine tool, textile and banking industries in order to analyse the effective demand for human resources. Those collaborating on the two studies included Reinhard Bahnmüller and Yuri Kazepov (Germany), Ida Regalia, Renata Semenza and Asher Colombo (Italy), Maïten Bell and Cecil Abattu (France), Andreu Lope, Martin Artiles, Xavier Coller, Fausto Miguelez and Angel Belzunegui (Spain).

6. Of course, stressing common trends entails neglecting differences which are profound, not only among countries but also among firms in the same country. Nevertheless, discussion of these general trends and their implications, albeit with all the caveats necessary, may prove fruitful for several reasons. First, these trends provide an overall picture (although one painted in overemphatic colours) of processes under way in various European countries. Second, they explain why the lack in certain countries of an institutional system as efficient as that in others may indeed be a problem, but one less important than has been assumed by the mainstream literature.

7. Indeed, whereas the *Konzertierte Aktion* of the period 1967–78 had no significant influence from this point of view, the central bank, as we have seen, played a crucial role from the mid-1970s onwards precisely because it was indirect.

References

Accornero, A. 1981. 'Sindacato e rivoluzione sociale: Il caso italiano degli anni '70', *Laboratorio Politico*, 4: 5–36.
  1988. 'Discontinuità capitalistiche e conseguenze sull'azione sindacale', in M. Regini (ed.), *La sfida della flessibilità*. Milan: Angeli, 222–34.
Addis, E. 1987. 'Banca d'Italia e politica monetaria: La riallocazione del potere fra stato, mercato e banca centrale', *Stato e Mercato*, 19: 73–95.
Alber, J. 1982. *Vom Armenhaus zum Wohlfahrtstaat: Analysen zur Entwicklung der Sozialversicherung in Westeuropa*. Frankfurt: Campus Verlag.
Amato, G. 1976. *Economia, politica e istituzioni in Italia*. Bologna: Il Mulino.
Anderson, C. W. 1977. 'Political Design and the Representation of Interests', *Comparative Political Studies*, 10.
Arrighetti, A. 1988. 'L'evoluzione dell'impresa manifatturiera alla luce della categoria di flessibilità', in M. Regini (ed.), *La sfida della flessibilità*. Milan: Angeli, 70–87.
Artoni, R. and Ranci Ortigosa, E. 1989. *La spesa pubblica per l'assistenza in Italia*. Milan: Angeli.
ASAP. 1989. *1989: Rapporto sui salari*. Milan: Angeli.
Ascoli, U. (ed.). 1984. *Welfare state all'italiana*. Bari: Laterza.
Baglioni, G. and Milani, R. (eds.). 1990. *La contrattazione collettiva nelle aziende industriali in Italia*. Milan: Angeli.
Bagnasco, A. 1988. *La costruzione sociale del mercato*. Bologna: Il Mulino.
Balbo, L. 1987. 'Family, Women, and the State: Notes Toward a Typology of Family Roles and Public Intervention', in C. Maier (ed.), *Changing Boundaries of the Political*. Cambridge University Press, 201–19.
Barca, F. and Magnani, M. 1989. *L'industria fra capitale e lavoro*. Bologna: Il Mulino.
Batstone, E. 1984. *Working Order: Workplace Industrial Relations in Britain over Two Decades*. Oxford: Basil Blackwell.
Bendix, R. 1964. *Nation-Building and Citizenship*. New York: Wiley.
Berger, S. (ed.). 1981. *Organizing Interests in Western Europe*. Cambridge University Press.
Berger, S. and Piore, M. 1980. *Dualism and Discontinuity in Industrial Societies*. Cambridge University Press.
Berta, G. and Michelsons, A. 1989. 'Il caso Olivetti' in M. Regini and C. Sabel (eds.), *Strategie di riaggiustamento industriale*. Bologna: Il Mulino, 133–70.

Blaas, W. 1992. 'The Swiss Model: Corporatism or Liberal Capitalism?' in J. Pekkarinen, M. Pohjola and B. Rowthorn (eds.), *Social Corporatism and Economic Performance*. Oxford: Oxford University Press, 363–76.

Bordogna, L. 1989. 'Il caso del Petrolchimico Montedison di Ferrara', in M. Regini and C. Sabel (eds.), *Strategie di riaggiustamento industriale*. Bologna: Il Mulino, 95–132.

Bordogna, L. and Provasi, G. 1984. *Politica, economia e rappresentanza degli interessi*. Bologna: Il Mulino.

Boyer, R. (ed.). 1986. *La flexibilité du travail en Europe*. Paris: La Découverte.

1988. 'Alla ricerca di alternative al fordismo: Gli anni ottanta', *Stato e Mercato*, 24: 387–423.

Brusco, S. 1986. 'Small Firms and Industrial Districts: The Experience of Italy', in D. Keeble and E. Wever (eds.), *New Firms and Regional Development in Europe*. London: Croom Helm, 184–202.

Butera, F. 1987. *Opzioni per il futuro del lavoro*. Milan: RSO, mimeo.

Calmfors, L. and Driffill, J. 1988. 'Centralization of Wage Bargaining', *Economic Policy*, 6: 13–61.

Cameron, D. 1984. 'Social Democracy, Corporatism, Labour Quiescence, and the Representation of Economic Interest in Advanced Capitalist Society', in J. Goldthorpe (ed.), *Order and Conflict in Contemporary Capitalism*. Oxford: Clarendon Press, 143–78.

Carrieri, M. and Donolo, C. 1986. *Il mestiere politico del sindacato*. Rome: Editori Riuniti.

Cassese, S. 1987. 'Stato ed economia: Il problema storico', in P. Lange and M. Regini (eds.), *Stato e regolazione sociale*. Bologna: Il Mulino, 45–52.

Catanzaro, R. 1983. 'Struttura sociale, sistema politico e azione collettiva nel mezzogiorno', *Stato e Mercato*, 8: 271–315.

Cavazza, F. and Graubard, S. (eds.). 1974. *Il caso italiano*. Milan: Garzanti.

Cella, G. P. 1989. 'Criteria of Regulation in Italian Industrial Relations: A Case of Weak Institutions', in P. Lange and M. Regini (eds.), *State, Market and Social Regulation*. Cambridge University Press, 167–85.

Chiesi, A. 1990. 'Un quadro di riferimento concettuale', *Democrazia e Diritto*, 1: 13–30.

Chiesi, A. and Martinelli, A. 1989. 'The Representation of Business Interests as a Mechanism of Social Regulation', in P. Lange and M. Regini (eds.), *State, Market and Social Regulation*. Cambridge University Press, 187–213.

Crouch, C. 1977. *Class Conflict and the Industrial Relations Crisis*. London: Heinemann.

1978. 'Inflation and the Political Organization of Economic Interests', in F. Hirsch and J. Goldthorpe (eds.), *The Political Economy of Inflation*. Cambridge Mass.: Harvard University Press, 217–39.

Crozier, M., Huntington, S. P. and Watanuki, J. 1975. *The Crisis of Democracy: Report on the Governability of Democracies to the Trilateral Commission*. New York: New York University Press.

Cutcher-Gershenfeld, J. 1991. 'The Impact on Economic Performance of a Transformation in Workplace Relations', *Industrial and Labor Relations Review*, 44 (2): 241–60.

Dente, B. 1985. *Governare la frammentazione*. Bologna: Il Mulino.

Dente, B. and Regonini, G. 1989. 'Politics and Policies in Italy', in P. Lange and M. Regini (eds.), *State, Market and Social Regulation*. Cambridge University Press, 51–79.

Dore, R. 1986. *Flexible Rigidities: Industrial Policy and Structural Adjustment in the Japanese Economy, 1970–1980*. Stanford, Calif.: Stanford University Press.

1987. *Taking Japan Seriously: A Confucian Perspective on Leading Economic Issues*. Stanford, Calif.: Stanford University Press.

Edwards, P., Hall, M., Hyman, R., Marginson, P., Sisson, K. Waddington, J. and Winchester, D. 1992. 'Great Britain: Still Muddling Through', in A. Ferner and R. Hyman (eds.), *Industrial Relations in the New Europe*. Oxford: Basil Blackwell, 1–68.

Epstein, G. and Schor, J. 1989. 'The Divorce of the Banca d'Italia and the Italian Treasury: A Case Study of Central Bank Independence', in P. Lange and M. Regini (eds.), *State, Market and Social Regulation*. Cambridge University Press, 147–64.

Espina, A. 1991. 'Politica de rentas en España', in F. Miguélez and C. Prieto (eds.), *Las relaciones laborales en España*. Madrid: Siglo XXI, 331–57.

Esping-Andersen, G. 1985. *Politics against Markets*. Princeton, N.J.: Princeton University Press.

1986. 'Stato sociale e attività economica: Tre rivoluzioni silenziose in attesa della quarta', in M. Regini (ed.), *Risposte alla crisi del welfare state: Ridurre o trasformare le politiche sociali?* Milan: Angeli, 17–24.

1987. 'Citizenship and Socialism: De-commodification and Solidarity in the Welfare State', in G. Esping-Andersen, M. Rein and L. Rainwater (eds.), *Stagnation and Renewal in Social Policy: The Rise and Fall of Policy Regimes*. Armonk, N.Y.: Sharpe, 78–101.

Faustini, G. 1990. 'Relazioni industriali e costo del lavoro alle soglie degli anni '90', *Politiche del Lavoro*, 10:191–201.

Ferrera, M. 1984. *Il welfare state in Italia*. Bologna: Il Mulino.

1989. 'Politics, Institutional Features and the Government of Industry', in P. Lange and M. Regini (eds.), *State, Market and Social Regulation*. Cambridge University Press, 111–27.

Flanagan, R., Soskice, D. and Ulman, L. 1984. *Unionism, Economic Stabilization and Incomes Policies: The European Experience*. Washington, D.C.: Brookings Institution.

Flora, P. (ed.). 1986. *Growth to Limits: The Western European Welfare States Since World War II*, 5 vols. Berlin: de Gruyter.

Flora, P. and Heidenheimer, A.J. (eds.). 1981. *The Development of Welfare States in Europe and America*. New Brunswick, N.J.: Transaction Books.

Gerschenkron, A. 1962. *Economic Backwardness in Historical Perspective*. Cambridge, Mass.: Harvard University Press.

Goetschy, J. and Rozenblatt, P. 1992. 'France: The Industrial Relations System at a Turning Point?' in A. Ferner and R. Hyman (eds.), *Industrial Relations in the New Europe*. Oxford: Basil Blackwell, 404–44.

Golden, M. 1988. *Labor Divided: Incomes Policies, Trade Unions and the Italian Communist Party*. Ithaca, N.Y.: Cornell University Press.

1993. 'The Dynamics of Trade Unionism and National Economic Performance,' *American Political Science Review*, 87 (2): 439–56.

Goldthorpe, J. (ed.). 1984. *Order and Conflict in Contemporary Capitalism.* Oxford: Clarendon Press.

1987. 'Problems of Political Economy after the Postwar Period', in C. Maier (ed.), *Changing Boundaries of the Political.* Cambridge University Press, 363–407.

Goldthorpe, J., Lockwood, D. Bechhofer, F. and Platt, J. 1968. *The Affluent Worker: Industrial Attitudes and Behaviour.* Cambridge University Press.

Granaglia, E. 1989. 'Public Intervention and Health Policy: An Analysis of Tendencies in Progress', in P. Lange and M. Regini (eds.), *State, Market and Social Regulation.* Cambridge University Press, 235–48.

Granovetter, M. 1985. 'Economic Action and Social Structure: The Problem of Embeddedness', *American Journal of Sociology,* 91 (3): 481–510.

Hall, P. 1986. *Governing the Economy: The Politics of State Intervention in Britain and France.* Cambridge: Polity Press.

1994. 'Central Bank Independence and Coordinated Wage Bargaining: Their Interaction in Germany and Europe', *German Politics and Society,* 31: 1–23.

Heclo, H. 1974. *Modern Social Politics in Britain and Sweden.* New Haven, Conn.: Yale University Press.

1978. 'Issue Networks and the Executive Establishment', in A. King (ed.), *The New American Political System.* Washington D.C.: American Enterprise Institute.

Hinrichs, K., Offe, C. and Wiesenthal, H. 1985, 'Crisi del welfare state e possibili alternative di ridistribuzione del lavoro', *Stato e Mercato,* 15: 397–422.

Hirschman, A. 1970. *Exit, Voice, and Loyalty.* Cambridge, Mass.: Harvard University Press.

Hyman, R. 1991. 'European Unions: Towards 2000', *Work, Employment and Society,* 5 (4): 621–39.

Jacobi, O., Keller, B. and Müller-Jentsch, W. 1992. 'Germany: Codetermining the Future', in A. Ferner and R. Hyman (eds.), *Industrial Relations in the New Europe.* Oxford: Basil Blackwell, 218–69.

Kalecki, M. 1943. 'Political Aspects of Full Employment', *Political Quarterly,* 14 (4): 322–31.

Katz, H. 1985. *Shifting Gears: Changing Labor Relations in the U.S. Automobile Industry.* Cambridge, Mass.: MIT Press.

Katzenstein, P. 1984. *Corporatism and Change: Austria, Switzerland and the Politics of Industry.* Ithaca, N.Y.: Cornell University Press.

Keeler, J. T. 1981. 'Corporatism and Official Union Hegemony: The Case of French Agricultural Syndicalism', in S. Berger (ed.), *Organizing Interests in Western Europe.* Cambridge University Press, 185–208.

Keynes, J. M. 1936. *The General Theory of Employment, Interest and Money.* London: Macmillan.

Kern, H. and Schumann, M. 1984. *Das Ende der Arbeitsteilung? Rationalisierung in der Industriellen Produktion.* Munich: Beck.

Kircheimer, O. 1966. 'The Transformation of the Western European Party System', in J. La Palombara and M. Weiner (eds.), *Political Parties and Political Development.* Princeton, N.J.: Princeton University Press, 177–200.

Kochan, T., Katz, H., and McKersie, R. 1986. *The Transformation of American Industrial Relations.* New York: Basic Books.

Korpi, W. 1978. *The Working Class in Welfare Capitalism: Work, Unions and Politics in Sweden.* London: Routledge & Kegan Paul.

1983. *The Democratic Class Struggle.* London: Routledge & Kegan Paul.

Korpi, W. and Shalev, M. 1980. 'Strikes, Power and Politics in the Western Nations, 1900–1976', in M. Zeitlin (ed.), *Political Power and Social Theory,* Vol. 1. Greenwich, Conn.: JAI Press, 301–34.

Lange, P. 1984a. *Union Democracy and Liberal Corporatism: Exit, Voice and Wage Regulation in Post-War Europe.* Ithaca, N.Y.: Cornell University Western Societies Program Monograph.

1984b 'Unions, Workers, and Wage Regulation: The Rational Bases of Consent', in J. Goldthorpe (ed.), *Order and Conflict in Contemporary Capitalism.* Oxford: Clarendon Press, 98–123.

Lange, P. and Garrett, J. 1985. 'The Politics of Growth: Strategic Interaction and Economic Performance in the Advanced Industrial Democracies, 1974–1980', *Journal of Politics,* 47 (3): 792–827.

Lange, P. and Regini, M. (eds.). 1989. *State, Market and Social Regulation: New Perspectives on Italy.* Cambridge University Press.

Lange, P. and Tarrow, S. (eds.). 1980. *Italy in Transition.* London: Frank Cass.

Lash, S. and Urry, J. 1987. *The End of Organized Capitalism.* Cambridge: Polity.

Lehmbruch, G. 1977. 'Liberal Corporatism and Party Government', *Comparative Political Studies,* 10 (1): 91–126.

1982. 'Introduction: Neo-corporatism in Comparative Perspective', in G. Lehmbruch and P. Schmitter (eds.), *Patterns of Corporatist Policy-Making.* London: Sage, 1–28.

Lehmbruch, G. and Schmitter, P. (eds.). 1982. *Patterns of Corporatist Policy-Making.* London: Sage.

Lenhardt, G. and Offe, C. 1977. 'Staatstheorie und Sozialpolitik', *Kölner Zeitschrift für Soziologie und Sozialpsychologie,* Sonderheft 19: 98–127.

Lindberg, L. and Maier, C. (eds.). 1985. *The Politics of Inflation and Economic Stagnation.* Washington, D.C.: Brookings Institution.

Lindblom, C. 1977. *Politics and Markets.* New York: Basic Books.

Locke, R. 1994. *Reconstituting the Italian Economy.* Ithaca, N.Y.: Cornell University Press.

Locke, R. and Negrelli, S. 1989. 'Il caso Fiat Auto', in M. Regini and C. Sabel (eds.), *Strategie di riaggiustamento industriale.* Bologna: Il Mulino, 61–94.

Lowi, T. J. 1972. 'Four Systems of Policy, Politics and Choice', *Public Administration Review,* 32 (4): 298–310.

Lutz, B. 1975. *Krise des Lohnanreizes.* Frankfurt: Europäische Verlagsanstalt.

Maier, C. (ed.). 1987. *Changing Boundaries of the Political.* Cambridge University Press.

Maraffi, M. 1987. 'Le politiche industriali', in G. Romagnoli (ed.), *Le relazioni fra amministrazione e sindacati,* Archivio ISAP 4. Milan: Giuffré, 1127–81.

Marin, B. 1983. 'Organizing Interests by Interest Organizations: Associational Prerequisites of Cooperation in Austria', *International Political Science Review,* 4 (2): 137–216.

Marsden, D. and Silvestre, J. J. 1990. *Wage Policy and European Integration.* Aix-en-Provence: LEST. London: LSE; mimeo.

Marshall, T. H. 1964. *Class, Citizenship, and Social Development.* Garden City, N.Y.: Doubleday.

Martin, A. 1979. 'The Dynamics of Change in a Keynesian Political Economy: The Swedish Case and Its Implications', in C. Crouch (ed.), *State and Economy in Contemporary Capitalism*. London: Croom Helm, 88–121.

Maurice, M., Sellier, F. and Silvestre, J. J. 1982. *Politique d'éducation et organisation industrielle en France et en Allemande*. Paris: PUF.

Mény, Y. and Wright, V. (eds.). 1987. *The Politics of Steel: Western Europe and the Steel Industry in the Crisis Years (1974–1984)*. Berlin: de Gruyter.

Miguélez, F. 1991. 'Las organizaciones sindicales', in F. Miguélez and C. Prieto (eds.), *Las relaciones laborales en España*. Madrid: Siglo XXI, 213–31.

Miguelez, F. and Prieto, C. (eds.). 1991. *Las relaciones laborales en España*. Madrid: Siglo XXI.

Money, J. 1992. 'The Decentralization of Collective Bargaining in Belgium, France and the United States', in M. Golden and J. Pontusson (eds.), *Bargaining for Change*. Ithaca, N.Y.: Cornell University Press, 77–108.

Negrelli, S. 1989. 'Il caso Italtel', in M. Regini and C. Sabel (eds.), *Strategie di riaggiustamento industriale*. Bologna: Il Mulino, 171–206.

O'Connor, J. 1973. *The Fiscal Crisis of the State*. New York: St. Martin's Press.

Offe, C. 1981. 'The Attribution of Public Status to Interest Groups: Observations on the W. German Case' in S. Berger (ed.), *Organizing Interests in Western Europe*. Cambridge University Press, 123–58.

1984. *Contradictions of the Welfare State*. London: Hutchinson.

1985. *Disorganized Capitalism*. Cambridge: Polity.

Ojeda Avilés, A. (ed.). 1990. *La concertación social tras la crisis*. Barcelona: Editorial Ariel.

Olson, M. 1965. *The Logic of Collective Action*. Cambridge, Mass.: Harvard University Press.

Ouchi, W. G. 1977. 'Markets, Bureaucracies and Clans', *Administrative Science Quarterly*, 25.

Paci, M. 1984. 'Il sistema di welfare italiano tra tradizione clientelare e prospettive di riforma', in U. Ascoli (ed.), *Welfare state all'italiana*. Bari: Laterza, 297–323.

1989. *Pubblico e privato nei moderni sistemi di welfare*. Naples: Liguori.

Panitch, L. 1977. 'The Development of Corporatism in Liberal Democracies', *Comparative Political Studies*, 10 (1): 61–90.

1980. 'Recent Theorizations of Corporatism: Reflections on a Growth Industry', *British Journal of Sociology*, 31 (2): 159–87.

Parri, L. 1987. 'Neo-corporatist Arrangements, "Konkordanz" and Direct Democracy: The Swiss Experience', in I. Scholten (ed.), *Political Stability and Neo-Corporatism*. London: Sage, 70–94.

Pasquino, G. 1986. 'Party Government in Italy: Achievements and Prospects', in R. Katz (ed.), *The American and European Experiences of Party Government*. Berlin: de Gruyter.

1989, 'Unregulated Regulators: Parties and Party Government', in P. Lange and M. Regini (eds.), *State, Market and Social Regulation*. Cambridge University Press, 29–50.

Pérez Diaz, V. 1987. *El retorno de la sociedad civil*. Madrid: Instituto de Estudios Economicos.

Perulli, P. 1989. 'Il distretto industriale di Modena', in M. Regini and C. Sabel (eds.), *Strategie di riaggiustamento industriale*. Bologna: Il Mulino, 243–82.

Pichierri, A. 1989. *Strategie contro il declino in aree di antica industrializzazione.* Torino: Rosenberg & Sellier.

Piore, M. and Sabel, C. 1984. *The Second Industrial Divide.* New York: Basic Books.

Piven, F. F. and Cloward, R. 1971. *Regulating the Poor.* New York: Random House.

Pizzorno, A. 1978. 'Political Exchange and Collective Identity in Industrial Conflict', in C. Crouch and A. Pizzorno (eds.), *The Resurgence of Class Conflict in Western Europe Since 1968.* London: Macmillan, 2: 277–98.

1981. 'Interests and Parties in Pluralism', in S. Berger (ed.), *Organizing Interests in Western Europe.* Cambridge University Press, 246–84.

Pizzorno, A., Reyneri, E., Regini, M. and Regalia, I. 1978. *Lotte operaie e sindacato: Il ciclo 1968–1972 in Italia.* Bologna: Il Mulino.

Polanyi, K. 1944. *The Great Transformation.* New York: Holt, Rinehart & Winston.

Pontusson, J. 1992. 'Unions, New Technology, and Job Redesign at Volvo and British Leyland', in M. Golden and J. Pontusson (eds.), *Bargaining for Change.* Ithaca, N.Y.: Cornell University Press, 277–306.

Przeworski, A. 1985. *Capitalism and Social Democracy.* Cambridge University Press.

Regalia, I. 1987. 'Le politiche del lavoro', in G. Romagnoli (ed.), *Le relazioni fra amministrazione e sindacati,* Archivio ISAP 4. Milan: Giuffré, 967–1043.

1989. 'L'area di Sesto S. Giovanni', in M. Regini and C. Sabel (eds.), *Strategie di riaggiustamento industriale.* Bologna: Il Mulino, 207–48.

Regalia, I. and Ronchi, R. 1988, 1989, 1990. *Le relazioni industriali nelle imprese lombarde.* Milan: IRES papers collana ricerche.

Regini, M. 1981. *I dilemmi del sindacato.* Bologna: Il Mulino.

1982. 'Changing Relationships Between Labour and the State in Italy: Towards a Neo-corporatist System?' in G. Lehmbruch and P. Schmitter (eds.), *Patterns of Corporatist Policy-Making.* London: Sage, 109–32.

1984. 'The Conditions for Political Exchange: How Concertation Emerged and Collapsed in Italy and Great Britain', in J. Goldthorpe (ed.), *Order and Conflict in Contemporary Capitalism.* Oxford: Clarendon Press, 126–42.

1987. 'Social Pacts in Italy', in I. Scholten (ed.), *Political Stability and Neo-Corporatism.* London: Sage, 195–215.

Regini, M. (ed.). 1992. *The Future of Labour Movements.* London: Sage.

Regini, M. and Sabel, C. (eds.). 1989. *Strategie di riaggiustamento industriale.* Bologna: Il Mulino.

Regonini, G. 1985. 'Le politiche sociali in Italia: Metodi di analisi', *Rivista Italiana di Scienza Politica,* 15 (3): 335–77.

1987. 'Le politiche pensionistiche', in G. Romagnoli (ed.), *Le relazioni fra amministrazione e sindacati,* Archivio ISAP 4. Milan: Giuffré, 1045–1126.

Reyneri, E. 1988. 'L'innovazione produttiva nella rete delle relazioni sociali', *Stato e Mercato,* 23: 147–76.

1989. 'The Italian Labor Market: Between State Control and Social Regulation', in P. Lange and M. Regini (eds.), *State, Market and Social Regulation.* Cambridge University Press, 129–45.

Richardson, J. (ed.). 1982. *Policy Styles in Western Europe.* London: Allen & Unwin.

Rimlinger, G. 1971. *Welfare Policy and Industrialization in Europe, America and Russia.* New York: Wiley.

Roca, J. 1991. 'La concertación social', in F. Miguélez and C. Prieto (eds.), *Las relaciones laborales en España.* Madrid: Siglo XXI, 361–77.

Rose, R. 1979. 'Ungovernability: Is There Fire Behind the Smoke?' *Political Studies*, 27 (3): 351–70.

1984. *Understanding Big Government*. London: Sage.

Ruesga S. 1991. 'La negociación colectiva', in F. Miguélez and C. Prieto (eds.), *Las relaciones laborales en España*. Madrid: Siglo XXI, 379–402.

Sabel, C. 1981. 'The Internal Politics of Trade Unions', in S. Berger (ed.), *Organizing Interests in Western Europe*. Cambridge University Press, 209–44.

1988. 'La flessibilità industriale in una prospettiva storico-comparativa: Alcuni esempi tedeschi e americani', in M. Regini (ed.), *La sfida della flessibilità*. Milan: Angeli, 41–54.

1989. 'Flexible Specialization and the Re-emergence of Regional Economies', in P. Hirst and J. Zeitlin (eds.), *Reversing Industrial Decline? Industrial Structure and Policy in Britain and Her Competitors*. New York: St. Martin's Press, 17–70.

Salvati, M. 1980. *Alle origini dell' inflazione italiana*. Bologna: Il Mulino.

1982. 'Strutture politiche ed esiti economici', *Stato e Mercato*, 4: 3–43.

Sartori, G. 1966. 'European Political Parties: The Case of Polarized Pluralism', in J. La Palombara and M. Weiner (eds.), *Political Parties and Political Development*. Princeton, N.J.: Princeton University Press, 137–76.

Scharpf, F. 1984. 'Economic and Institutional Constraints of Full-Employment Strategies: Sweden, Austria and W. Germany, 1973–1982', in J. Goldthorpe (ed.), *Order and Conflict in Contemporary Capitalism*. Oxford: Clarendon Press, 257–90.

1991. *Crisis and Choice in European Social Democracy*. Ithaca, N.Y.: Cornell University Press.

Schmitter, P. 1974. 'Still the Century of Corporatism?' *Review of Politics*, 36 (1): 85–131.

1981. 'Interest Intermediation and Regime Governability in Contemporary W. Europe and N. America', in S. Berger (ed.), *Organizing Interests in Western Europe*. Cambridge University Press, 285–327.

Schmitter, P. and Lehmbruch, G. (eds.). 1979. *Trends Toward Corporatist Intermediation*. London: Sage.

Scholten, I. 1987. 'Corporatism and the Neo-liberal Backlash in the Netherlands', in I. Scholten (ed.), *Political Stability and Neo-Corporatism*. London: Sage, 120–52.

Selznick, P. 1957. *Leadership in Administration*. New York: Harper & Row.

Shalev, M. 1983. 'The Social-Democratic Model and Beyond', *Comparative Social Research*, 6.

Shonfield, A. 1965. *Modern Capitalism*. Oxford: Oxford University Press.

Simon, H. 1947. *Administrative Behaviour*. New York: Macmillan.

Skidelsky, R. 1979. 'The Decline of Keynesian Politics', in C. Crouch (ed.), *State and Economy in Contemporary Capitalism*. London: Croom Helm, 55–87.

Skocpol, T. 1985. 'Bringing the State Back In: Strategies of Analysis in Current Research', in P. Evans, D. Rueschemeyer and T. Skocpol (eds.), *Bringing the State Back In*. Cambridge University Press, 3–43.

Skocpol, T. and Ikenberry, J. 1985. 'The Political Formation of the American Welfare State', in M. Rein and L. Rainwater (eds.), *Stagnation and Renewal: The Rise and Fall of Social Policy Regimes*. Armonk, N.Y.: Sharpe.

Soskice, D. 1978. 'Strike Waves and Wage Explosions, 1968–1970: An Economic Interpretation', in C. Crouch and A. Pizzorno (eds.), *The Resurgence of Class Conflict in Western Europe Since 1968*. London: Macmillan, 2: 221–46.

1990a. 'Reinterpreting Corporatism and Explaining Unemployment: Coordinated and Non-Coordinated Market Economies', in R. Brunetta and C. Dell'Aringa (eds.), *Markets, Institutions and Corporations: Labour Relations and Economic Performance*. New York: New York University Press, 170–211.

1990b. 'Wage Determination: The Changing Role of Institutions in Advanced Industrialized Countries', *Oxford Review of Economic Policy*, 6 (4): 36–61.

Stephens, J. 1979. *The Transition from Capitalism to Socialism*. London: Macmillan Press.

Streeck, W. 1984. 'Neo-corporatist Industrial Relations and the Economic Crisis in West Germany', in J. Goldthorpe (ed.), *Order and Conflict in Contemporary Capitalism*. Oxford: Clarendon Press, 291–314.

1987. 'The Uncertainties of Management in the Management of Uncertainty: Employers, Labor Relations and Industrial Adjustment in the 1980s', *Work, Employment and Society*. 1 (3): 281–308.

1989. 'Skills and the Limits of Neo-Liberalism: The Enterprise of the Future as a Place of Learning', *Work, Employment and Society*. 3 (1): 89–104.

1991. 'More Uncertainties: West German Unions Facing 1992', *Industrial Relations*, 30 (3): 317–49.

1992. *Social Institutions and Economic Performance*. London: Sage.

1994. 'Pay Restraint Without Incomes Policy: Constitutionalized Monetarism and Industrial Unionism in Germany', in R. Boyer and R. Dore (eds.), *The Return of Incomes Policy?* London: Pinter.

Streeck, W. and Schmitter, P. 1985. 'Community, Market, State – and Associations? The Prospective Contribution of Interest Governance to Social Order', *European Sociological Review*, 1 (2): 119–38.

Swenson, P. 1989. *Bringing Capital Back In, or Corporatism Reconsidered: Employer Power in Denmark, Sweden and Italy*. Philadelphia: University of Pennsylvania, mimeo.

Tarantelli, E. 1986. *Economia politica del lavoro*. Torino: Utet.

Tarrow, S. 1990. *Democrazia e disordine: Movimenti di protesta e politica in Italia, 1965–1975*. Bari: Laterza.

Terry, M. 1985. 'Shop Stewards and Management: Collective Bargaining as Co-operation', in O. Jacobi et al. (eds.), *Technological Change, Rationalisation and Industrial Relations*. London: Croom Helm, 161–75.

Thelen, K. 1991. *Union of Parts: Labor Politics in Postwar Germany*. Ithaca, N.Y.: Cornell University Press.

Titmuss, R. 1974. *Social Policy: An Introduction*. London: Allen & Unwin.

Trigilia, C. 1986. *Grandi partiti e piccole imprese*. Bologna: Il Mulino.

1989. 'Il distretto industriale di Prato', in M. Regini and C. Sabel (eds.), *Strategie di riaggiustamento industriale*. Bologna: Il Mulino, 283–333.

1992. *Sviluppo senza autonomia*. Bologna: Il Mulino.

Turner, L. 1992. *Democracy at Work: Changing World Markets and the Future of Labor Unions*. Ithaca, N.Y.: Cornell University Press.

Ulman, L. and Flanagan, R. 1971. *Wage Restraint: A Study of Incomes Policies in Western Europe*. Berkeley: University of California Press.

Valdés Dal-Ré, F. 1991. 'Le système espagnol de relations professionelles', in C. Guitton, M. Maruani and E. Reynaud (eds.), *L'Emploi en Espagne*. Paris: Syros, 45–64.

Visser, J. 1992. 'The Strength of Union Movements in Advanced Capitalist Democracies: Social and Organizational Variations', in M. Regini (ed.), *The Future of Labour Movements*. London: Sage, 17–52.

Weir, M. 1987. 'Idee e politica: l'adesione al keynesismo in Gran Bretagna e negli Stati Uniti', *Stato e Mercato,* 20: 179–213.

Wilensky, H. 1975. *The Welfare State and Equality.* Berkeley: University of California Press.

Williamson, O. 1975. *Markets and Hierarchies: Analysis and Antitrust Implications.* New York: Free Press.

Womack, J., Jones, D. and Roos, D. 1990. *The Machine That Changed the World.* New York: HarperCollins.

Index